THE
PORTABLE
STANFORD

**PUBLISHED BY THE
STANFORD ALUMNI ASSOCIATION**

CORY AQUINO

AND THE PEOPLE OF THE PHILIPPINES

Claude A. Buss

STANFORD ALUMNI ASSOCIATION
STANFORD, CALIFORNIA

THE PORTABLE STANFORD is a series
publication of the Stanford Alumni
Association. Each book is an original
work written expressly for this series by
a member of the Stanford University
faculty. The PS series is designed to bring
the widest possible sampling of Stanford's
intellectual resources into the homes of
alumni. It includes books based on
current research as well as books that
deal with philosophical issues, which by
their nature reflect to a greater degree the
personal views of their authors.

THE PORTABLE STANFORD
Stanford Alumni Association
Bowman Alumni House
Stanford, California 94305

Library of Congress Catalog Card
Number 87-060413
ISBN: 0-916318-25-7
ISBN: 0-916318-24-9 pbk.

This is the story of a bloodless revolution,
inspired by a widow
and her martyred husband,
that drove a discredited ruler into exile
and gave a nation and its people a fresh
start in restoring law and order,
reviving the economy, and
returning to the ways of democracy.

CONTENTS

5

The Challenge of Military Reform / 83

Law: Marcos Style ■ The Erosion of the Military Tradition ■ The Military Under Marcos ■ The Aquino Revival ■ The Complexity of the Challenge

6

The Moro Rebellion / 105

The Marcos Policies ■ Aquino and the Moros

7

The Communist Insurgency: the NPA / 117

Origins of Philippine Communism ■ The Mounting Threat ■ Communism: Philippine Style ■ Changing Strategies ■ Cory and the Communists ■ Renewed Violence

8

Foreign Relations: Before Aquino / 137

The Colonial Heritage ■ World War II ■ The Dark Side of Independence ■ "Special Relations" ■ The Rise of Nationalism ■ Foreign Relations Under Marcos ■ Renegotiating the Military Bases ■ Reassessment of U.S. Policy

9

Foreign Relations: The Aquino Scenario / 163

A New Approach to Foreign Affairs ■ Working with Japan and ASEAN ■ Relations with the United States ■ The U.S. Shifts its Stance ■ U.S. Economic and Military Assistance ■ The Military Bases ■ The Road Ahead

Suggested Reading / 191

About the Author / 197

Credits / 199

PREFACE
AND
ACKNOWLEDGMENTS

A new personality rocketed into the consciousness of the world when on February 7, 1986, Corazon ("Cory") Aquino, who described herself as a "simple housewife," was elected president of the Philippines, driving into exile an aging and ailing ruler who for more than a decade had exercised total power and assumed total responsibility for his country. In the course of a unique revolution lasting four days, people all over the world witnessed, thanks to television, the spectacular triumph of the human spirit over the armed might of the faded dictator. Americans joined in the enthusiastic hurrahs for the Filipino people and showed a new interest in the fate of the nation that for half a century had been an American colony.

This book tells how Corazon Aquino came to be president of the Philippines, how she brought new life to her people, and how she made a fresh start in bringing back democracy, reviving the economy, reforming the military, suppressing rebellion, countering the communist insurgents, and restoring the Philippines to its honored place in the family of nations. The adoption of a new constitution on February 2, 1987 not only confirmed the popular mandate that brought her to power but gave her the promise of another five years in office to continue the work she had so courageously begun.

As seen in historical perspective, the transition time from Marcos to Aquino was exceedingly brief, allowing little time for the new president to prepare for the enormous tasks ahead. She nevertheless demolished the authoritarian Marcos regime with incredible speed and thoroughness. Her indomitable will, the raw courage of her followers, the support of the church, and the defection of the military gave a new dimension to the concept of revolution and a new image to the people of the Philippines.

Once in office President Aquino rapidly and impressively grew in stature to meet the demands on her. Although she lacked previous executive experience, she nevertheless performed like a seasoned veteran. She listened to everyone but made her own judgments. Refusing to be cowed by the new opposition of the Right or the Left, she was accused by her political rivals of many faults and mistakes—weakness, naiveté, procrastination, favoritism, and hypocrisy—but only history will tell whether she or they are correct.

This much is sure. She has stirred up the Filipinos' pride in themselves. Sincerely dedicated to the people's welfare, she has worked hard and kept the faith, accomplishing much in a single year. Watching her public performance in February 1987, as I had a year earlier, I can testify that she has lost none of her magic with the crowds. The wild cheers of "Coree! Coree!" constantly interrupt her speeches.

She will do her best to fulfill the hopes that she has aroused, and to use all her talent to avoid the inevitable pitfalls that lie ahead. If she fails, the consequences will be catastrophic.

Americans were given a slight glimpse of her charisma in her appearance before the U.S. Congress—perhaps the toughest audience in the world. Although the U.S. government will pursue common goals with whatever administration the Filipinos choose for themselves, Cory's continued success matters a great deal to Americans. Here is a president of the Philippines with values that we share and commitments to policies that we respect. The prospects for peace and cooperation are bright as long as she occupies the presidential palace in Manila.

In writing this book I hope to contribute to mutual understanding between the peoples of our two countries. For nearly half a century, since the day in January 1941 when I began my duties as executive assistant to the U.S. High Commissioner Francis B. Sayre in Manila, the Philippines has been my second home. For nearly a year I worked with other Americans to help President Quezon prepare his country for the coming war. As the senior American official left behind to face the Japanese when war finally came, I was interned in Manila, transferred to Tokyo, and eventually repatriated on the exchange ship *Gripsholm*.

Since that experience, the Philippines naturally has been very much a part of my life. I have made innumerable trips to the Philippines and have served twice as a Fulbright exchange professor at the University of the Philippines. I have met and discussed politics with every president of the Philippines, beginning with President Quezon. I have many Filipino friends with whom I argue constantly, with vigor and I hope with mutual respect. Conversations with them are, I am sure, woven into many pages of this Philippine story. To mention their names is also to absolve them from responsibility for any of my ideas. With special fondness, I think of Teddy Locsin, Sr., S.P. Lopez, and the dynamic F. Sionil ("Frankie") Jose.

Through the years, I have culled ideas from Americans who share my interest in and love for the Philippines. From Stanford University days, I recognize my debt of gratitude to Clifton and Nancy Forster, Paul Hanna, Joann Lewinsohn, Milton Meyer, and David Sturtevant. Writing again for the Portable Stanford series is taking another precious trip down memory lane with respected colleagues and a host of students. While at San Jose State, my Philippine experience was enriched by my colleagues Gerry Wheeler, Lela Noble, and my friend from the southland, Mike Onorato.

In teaching Asian Area Studies in the National Security Affairs Department of the U.S. Naval Postgraduate School in Monterey, it has been of great benefit to discuss the Philippines with my associates Pat Parker, Sherman Blandin, Boyd Huff, Frank Teti, Ed Laurance, Don Daniels, Ed Olsen, Harlan Jencks, Steve Jurika, and Jim Tritten. My thanks to all of them for their help and inspiration.

I have found intellectual stimulation and comradeship at Monterey in such students as Bob Brower, Hank Carde, Joe Bouchard, Dennis Fowler, Joe Menendez, Jack Carpenter, Joe Mazzufro, George Steuber, Lance Gatling, Bruce Brockhagen, Tom Shubert, Don Cann (of Siam), Neal Anderson, Bob Howell, Mark O'Neill, Joe Northrup, Rich Curasi,Tom Peterman, Steve Sciacchitano, Gary Porfert, Rick Saccone, Randy Larsen, and Dave Rich. All these officers have served in the

Philippines, elsewhere in Southeast Asia, on ships at sea, or in the skies above, and at one time or another have been helpful.

In the last trying, exciting days of the presidential succession from Marcos to Aquino, friends on both sides of the issues did their best to keep my views in balance. I am deeply grateful to Teddy Locsin, Jr., Alex Melchor, Ditos Bondoc, Vince Chuidian, Jolly Benitez, Helen Benitez, Ray Gregorio, Hezel Gacutan, Blas Ople, Raul Manglapus, and Inday Arcenas. On repeated occasions, I was received by President and Mrs. Marcos. As an ardent follower of Cory on the campaign trail, I frequently exchanged views with my interesting companions Al Ravenholt, Guy Pauker, Stan Karnow, Bob Shaplen, and Carl Mydans. Ambassador Bosworth and his staff were always extremely helpful. In the course of the year with which this book is primarily concerned, I made four trips to the Philippines: during the snap election of February 1986; at the end of the new government's first hundred days in May; while the constitution was under discussion in September; and at the time of the plebiscite in February 1987.

For assistance in the preparation of this manuscript, I am happy to make some very special acknowledgments: to Don Jagoe, my indispensable aide, research assistant, and traveling companion on two trips to Manila; to Miriam Miller, the capable and charming editor of the Portable Stanford series, for patience and tolerance far beyond the call of duty; to Betty Oates of the Hoover Institution and to Kathleen Jordan of the Portable Stanford, who performed miracles of their own in converting my hunt and peck typing into computerese; and to Gayle Hemenway of the Portable Stanford for transforming the manuscript into a book. I wish also to thank Edith Coliver, longtime representative of the Asia Foundation in the Philippines, for giving me the benefit of her criticisms and suggestions.

Finally, I want my family—my wife, Evelyn, her sister, Ruth, and my daughter, Lynne—to know how much I appreciate their love and support, without which this hectic year would not have been possible.

It goes without saying that in this book I speak for no one but myself. No government official in either the United States or the Philippines is in any way responsible for anything I have written. If anyone finds anything inaccurate or misleading I hope he or she will take pen in hand and set me straight.

Claude Buss

Palo Alto, California

ABBREVIATIONS

ABC	Anti-Bases Coalition
ADB	Asia Development Bank
AFP	Armed Forces of the Philippines
AID	American Agency for International Development
ASA	Association of Southeast Asia
ASEAN	Association of Southeast Asian Nations
BMA	Bangsa Moro Army
CBCP	Catholic Bishops Conference of the Philippines
CDCP	Construction and Development Corporation of the Philippines
COMELEC	Committee on Elections
CPP	Communist Party of the Philippines
Concom	Constitutional Commission
IMF	International Money Fund
INP	Integrated National Police
JUSMAG	Joint U.S. Military Advisory Group
KBL	Kilusang Bagong Lipunan (New Society Movement)
Laban	Lakas ng Bayan (Cory's political party)
MBA	Military Bases Agreement
MIM	Muslim Independence Movement
MNLF	Moro National Liberation Front
Metrocom	Metropolitan Command
NAFP	New Armed Forces of the Philippines
NAMFREL	National Movement for Free Elections
NASUTRA	National Sugar Trading Company
NBI	National Bureau of Investigation
NDF	National Democratic Front
NEDA	National Economic Development Authority
NISA	National Intelligence and Security Authority
NPA	New People's Army
OICs	Officers in Charge
PAL	Philippine Air Lines
PC	Philippine Constabulary
PCA	Philippine Coconut Authority
PCGG	Presidential Commission on Good Government
PCGR	Presidential Commission on Government Reorganization
PCHR	Presidential Commission on Human Rights
PCO	Presidential Commitment Order
PDA	Preventive Detention Action
PDP	Philippine Democratic Party
PHILCAG	Philippine Civil Action Group
PHILSUCOM	Philippine Sugar Commission
PKP	Partido Komunista ng Pilipinas (the original Communist Party of the Philippines)
PNB	Party ng Bayan (the Bayan Party)
PSC	Presidential Security Command
UCPB	United Coconut Planters Bank
UNICOM	United Coconut Mills
UNIDO	United National Democratic Organization
USIA	United States Information Agency
ZOPFAN	Zone of Peace, Freedom, and Neutrality

WHAT
THIS BOOK
IS ABOUT

The plan of this book is extremely simple: to place the events leading to the fall of President Marcos and the rise of President Aquino in the context of Philippine history. Although it does full justice, I hope, to the high drama of the People's Revolution, it is mainly concerned with the problems of the present government in reviving the economy, putting down the communist insurgency, and restoring democracy. It stresses the importance of a friendly and cooperative Philippines to the United States and to the entire free world.

As we explore Philippine history, searching for the roots of President Aquino's ideas and for those factors in the evolving political environment that eventually exploded into the People's Revolution, it will become clear that the ambivalence in the attitude of Filipinos toward the United States, so clearly discernible among the members of the Aquino cabinet, is as old as the Philippine-American relationship itself.

Every president of the independent Philippines has had to face the same endemic economic problems that face President Aquino. The inherent contradictions between the behavior patterns of Philippine society and the demands of an effective democratic government, with which the present government must contend, contributed to the downfall of every one of Mrs. Aquino's predecessors, including Marcos.

A capsulized description of the Marcos era shows the progressive steps by which Marcos deliberately discarded the principles and practices of democracy and proclaimed martial law. Neither total power and total responsibility nor consitutional authoritarianism were any more successful than the traditional patterns of Philippine democracy in giving the people the security and standard of living they had a right to expect. By the time Cory's husband, Benigno ("Ninoy") Aquino, was assassinated, the nation's distress had prepared the ground for a people's revolution.

The transition period between Ninoy's assassination on August 21, 1983, and the snap election of February 7, 1986, seen in historical perspective, was exceedingly brief. At the outset, the position of President Marcos seemed impregnable: He controlled the armed forces, the political apparatus that ruled the country, the national finances, and the press. His opposition was cowed and divided. But as his health declined, his political acumen diminished, and his economic schemes failed, the tide of popular protest rose relentlessly against him.

The incredible story of the Philippine revolution defies all precedent and probability. The indomitable will of the leader, the courage of her followers, the support of the church, and the defection of the military gave "revolution" a new meaning and the Philippine people a new image.

Having achieved an unprecedented victory, President Aquino embarked on a strenuous effort to restore democracy and free enterprise to the Philippines. On assuming office, her task was to dismantle the machinery of martial law, replace the Marcos appointees with popularly elected officials, and mold her disparate followers into a cooperative administrative organization. In giving the country a temporary constitution, she created a new government structure and put in operation a responsible system of democratic elections. She had to placate her foes on the right and on the left. She had to preserve the rights of a loyal opposition without completely derailing the governing process. Hers was the age-old problem of reconciling the personal interest of officials with the public welfare, and of getting things done without resort to favoritism and graft.

In the economic sphere she was forced to cope with the problems of poverty and the tremendous gap between the very rich and the masses of the poor. She was challenged to release the energies and talents of all Filipinos to put the nation back on the road to progress. Her aim was to rely on private enterprise and the free market for national development and to confine the power of the state to its role as guardian of social justice. The fundamentals of her economic program were to be land reform and rapid industrialization—and as much relief as she could get from the enormous burden of debt that Marcos left her.

The most urgent task of the contemporary Philippines is the restoration of law and order. Never have the police and the armed forces been so numerous, nor criminality more rampant and insurgency more threatening. With the help of her new and reformed armed forces, the President wants *in her own way* to put an end to the Moro rebellion and the communist insurgency. She is dedicated to the proposition that it is better to eradicate the roots of rebellion than merely to kill the rebels. She believes that policies of reconciliation, including a cease-fire and amnesty, hold out the best hope for reducing the strength of the communists. In spite of criticism at home and abroad she is convinced that resorting to force requires a strong moral justification. If reconciliation fails to win rebels and insurgents, she will fight them with all the means at her disposal.

An analysis of the background of President Aquino's thoughts and actions in foreign relations shows that, like every other Filipino, she is a genuine patriot and consequently a strong nationalist. She shares the national determination to get rid of the last vestiges of the colonial mentality, and the lingering but widespread resentment against the indignities that most Filipinos feel they suffered when the United States relinquished sovereignty over its former colony.

President Marcos pursued a philosophy of foreign relations that from a Filipino point of view seems eminently sensible. In order to reduce an embarrassing dependence on special relations with the United States, and in order to increase the Filipino sense of respectable independence, Marcos led the Philippines into closer relations with its Asian neighbors, with Australia and Japan, and with the socialist countries, including China and the Soviet Union. Although he flirted with ideas of non-alignment and a zone of peace, freedom, and neutrality for Southeast Asia, he could not escape his reliance on the United States for military support and economic assistance.

Mrs. Aquino, however, lends her own touch to the conduct of foreign relations. She, too, is sensitive to the implications of the geographic location of the Philippines—off the coast of Asia—and to the historical heritage of the close ties between the Philippines and the United States. In light of the fact that for so many years the United States was the staunchest supporter of the authoritarian Marcos regime, she not surprisingly takes with a grain of salt American preachments about freedom and democracy. She is by no means anti-American, although some of her closest colleagues seem to be very much so. Having lived in the United States for many years and under varied circumstances, she understands the United States and American politics far better than most Filipinos. Her upright character, her direct manner, and her aversion to bluff and bluster stand her in good stead as she deals with the United States on the controversial issues of trade and aid, American investments in the Philippines, and the renewal of the Military Bases Agreement.

At least two tentative conclusions emerge from the course of Corazon Aquino's brief political career: (1) at this juncture she appears as the best and last hope for a democratic Philippines, and (2) the prospects for harmonious and mutually advantageous Philippine-American relations are favorable.

As long as Marcos was in office, the feelings of each country toward the other were dangerously polarized. Within the Philippines, articulate nationalists were becoming increasingly bitter in their anti-Americanism. In the United States, the sentiment was growing that nothing about the Philippines was of any value whatsoever to the Americans except the military bases. The outlook was grim for a mutually agreeable settlement of the inevitable controversies over economic and security matters.

The new president's levelheadedness has halted both trends. Without fanfare, her attitudes and actions have dulled the fanaticism of her most ardent nationalist supporters. By her courageous conduct and dignified bearing, she has convinced even the toughest Americans that there is a great deal more to the Philippines than Subic Bay and Clark Field. Philippine-American arguments over trade and aid, claims and debts, investments, the multi-nationals, mutual security, and the military bases are bound to continue, but the chances of reaching amicable compromises are infinitely improved as long as Cory is at the helm of the Philippine ship of state.

In writing this book, I hope to contribute to a better understanding of the existing state of affairs in the Philippines. If we Americans have an adequate appreciation of the magnitude of the difficulties facing the Aquino administration, we will not be misled into expecting quick and miraculous improvements in their domestic affairs. And we will not be inclined to lose our patience when Filipinos adopt in their own interest foreign policies that run counter to our own.

Because our two nations, the United States and the Philippines, have common goals and perceive common dangers, I believe that good relations between us are essential for mutual security, and for the welfare of the Southeast Asia region. It is in the American interest to give the government of the Philippines our fullest support—by which I do not mean handouts that demean the giver and insult the receiver. The support I have in mind is identified more with attitude than with the dollar value assigned to military and economic assistance. The *amount* of help is less important than the willingness to cooperate that it symbolizes.

Since their People's Revolution, the Filipinos feel very good about themselves. Their growing pride, and their extreme sensitivity to the enormous differences in wealth and power between the United States and the Philippines, demand that Americans make strong efforts to understand Filipino points of view. To foster harmonious policies in economics and in security issues will require compromise and tolerance on both sides. The best way to retain Filipino faith in the United States and American confidence in the Philippines is to face our differences frankly, and in a spirit of determination to preserve all that has been good in our past relationship.

1

"In a revolution there can
really be no victors, only victims.
We do not have to destroy
in order to build."

Benigno ("Ninoy") Aquino

THE
AQUINO
DRAMA BEGINS

For as long as Ferdinand Marcos dominated Philippine politics, Benigno "Ninoy" Aquino was his most formidable opponent. The son of a wealthy landowner who had served in the cabinets of both President Quezon and President Laurel, Ninoy was the equal of Marcos in charisma and in the art of Philippine politics. When a mere eighteen years old, he had won a fair amount of public acclaim for his coverage of the war in Korea for the *Manila Times*. His first major national recognition came as the newspaper reporter who induced Luis Taruc, the Huk leader, to surrender to President Magsaysay.

In 1954, one month shy of his twenty-second birthday, Ninoy married Corazon "Cory" Cojuangco, also from his native province. The couple honeymooned in the United States, where his bride had studied from her second year in high school through her college days. From the beginning, Cory's destiny was inseparably linked with that of her husband. In Ninoy's first campaign for mayor of Concepcion, his hometown in Tarlac some 50 miles north of Manila, she learned from him how to talk to people and how to address a crowd. She watched the local speakers, who were unschooled and unlettered but

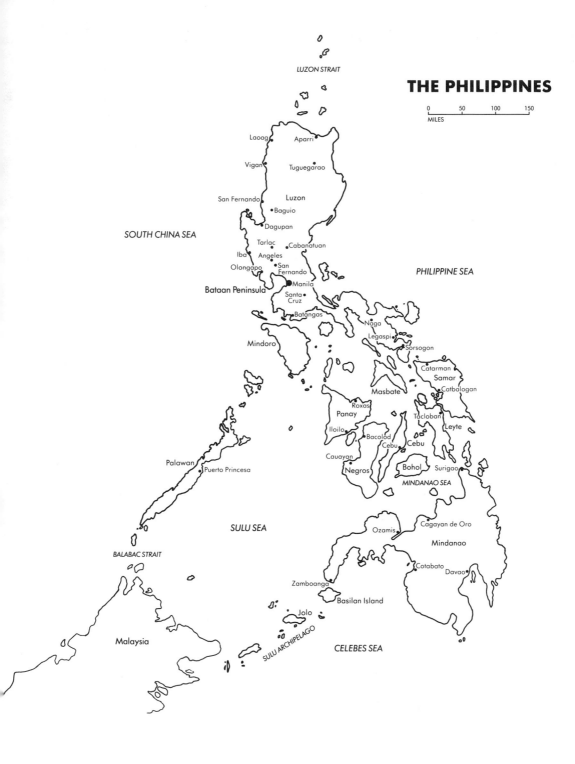

THE PHILIPPINES

0   50   100   150
MILES

LUZON STRAIT

SOUTH CHINA SEA

PHILIPPINE SEA

Laoag
Aparri
Vigan
Tuguegarao
San Fernando
Luzon
Baguio
Dagupan
Tarlac
Cabanatuan
Iba
Angeles
Olongapo
San Fernando
Manila
Bataan Peninsula
Santa Cruz
Batangas
Naga
Legaspi
Mindoro
Sorsogon
Catarman
Samar
Masbate
Catbalogan
Roxas
Tacloban
Panay
Leyte
Iloilo
Bacolod
Cebu
Cebu
Cauayan
Bohol
Surigao
Negros
MINDANAO SEA

Palawan
Puerto Princesa

SULU SEA

Cagayan de Oro
Ozamis
Mindanao

BALABAC STRAIT

Cotabato
Davao

Zamboanga
Basilan Island

Jolo
Malaysia
SULU ARCHIPELAGO
CELEBES SEA

riveting. They could hold an audience for hours, because they could put their points across in the form of stories. They would tell stories from the Bible, from mythology, or from popular folklore. From them she learned the technique of talking in parable—the technique of Christ, still effective after two thousand years.

Ninoy gave up his newspaper career to become a gentleman farmer. Running his sugar plantation as a model agribusiness, he became a highly successful entrepreneur. At the same time, he pushed forward with his political ambitions. As mayor of Concepcion, he commuted every day to Manila, learning about national politics as a member of President Magsaysay's staff. After Magsaysay's death, Ninoy continued on the staff of President Garcia until he was appointed governor of Tarlac. Thanks largely to his own hard work, his common sense in dealing with social problems, and his good relations with the American Agency for International Development (AID), Tarlac grew to become one of the most stable and prosperous provinces in the Philippines.

By a twist in political fortunes, at just about the time Ninoy deserted the Nacionalista Party to join the victorious Liberals under President Macapagal, Marcos deserted the Liberals to seek the presidency under the Nacionalista banner. The common practice of switching parties was not a matter of principle or ideology; it was merely a reassessment of one's chances to win an election. At every step of the way, Marcos and Aquino were on a collision course. Aquino thought of Marcos as a political phony, while Marcos called Aquino a "Huk-lover" and a "commie-coddler."

For his first six years in Malacañang, Marcos was opposed by Aquino, who served as the spokesman and secretary general of the oppositionist Liberal Party. Against heavy odds, Aquino was elected to the Senate in 1967. His most enthusiastic campaigners included his mother, Dona Aurora, and his wife, Cory. Constantly urging her son to "fight, boy, fight," his mother concentrated on the church. Cory stumped for him in factories and in town plazas on fiesta days. From the moment of his election to the Senate, Aquino attracted a following comparable to that of Marcos and was generally accepted as the man most likely to succeed to the presidency.

These early years of the Marcos-Aquino rivalry were years of education for Cory. Her own home was the rendezvous for partisan friends; her evenings out gave her a foretaste of the scheming, intrigue, and infighting that were the essence of Philippine political

Marcos seized the presses of the *Philippines Free Press* before this September 1972 issue was allowed to hit the streets.

life. The issues of land reform, poverty, industrialization, and communist insurgency became as familiar to her as to her husband. And as she listened to his views, they became her own.

In Marcos's eyes, Ninoy was the man most feared as his political enemy. On the day that martial law was proclaimed, the *Philippines Free Press* carried a cover page cartoon showing Ninoy in the cross hairs of a rifle, implying that Marcos was out to get him. The *Free Press* was shut down before the cartoon could reach the streets, and its publisher, Teodoro Locsin, was among those who, with Ninoy, were immediately carted off to prison.

For seven years and seven months—between 1972 and 1980—Ninoy, under sentence of death by a military tribunal for alleged subversion, languished in solitary confinement in a military prison. Cory was allowed to visit her husband once a week. She dates her central ideas of politics to those bittersweet moments together when two hearts beat as one, two minds thought as one. Seven years of separation, and the subsequent martyrdom of her husband, was the price she was forced to pay for her political education!

On May 8, 1980, Marcos granted Ninoy medical leave to go to the United States for emergency heart bypass surgery. While in the United States with his wife and five children, Ninoy sharpened his ideas about the Philippines and planned his own future course of action. He expounded his views in oral testimony before a U.S. congressional committee on June 23, 1983, just two months before his assassination. "The bloodletting in the Philippines must stop," he told the congressmen. "This madness must cease. We must forget our hurts and bitterness and let sanity, reason, and above all love of country prevail during our gravest hour."

DETERMINATION AND FAITH

No one was more aware than Ninoy of the suffering of his countrymen. These are his words:

> Millions of Filipinos are against the repressive dictatorship, rampant military abuses, runaway corruption, and gross mismanagement of the economy. Thousands of communist-led insurgents are engaging government forces all over our nation, thousands of Muslim secessionists are active in the southern Philippines, and thousands of Catholic priest-led

Ifugao tribesmen are on the warpath resisting eviction from their ancestral villages. And in the slums of the crowded cities, noncommunist, middle class-led urban guerrillas continue to recruit, train, and resupply their cells.

He believed, however, that the dictatorship would end only when Marcos died.

To his own rhetorical question, "Why is there no revolution, no cataclysmic explosion?" he replied, "One has to understand the dominant trait of the Filipino, which is both his strength and his weakness. Call it superstition or folk religion, but the Filipino fanatically believes in a supreme, divine law-giver that ordains all the affairs of men. A just God in his own season will eventually take care of everything. The irreplaceable Filipino phrase that captures all the nuances of this trait is *Bahala Na*, which means *Bath Allah* [God] *Na* [will take care]."

Regarding Marcos, Ninoy said, "A very calculating man, Marcos would rather persuade before he bribes, bribe before he threatens, threaten before he arrests, arrest before he kills." Ninoy was convinced that the end of Marcos's reign was near because of his ill health, his waning power, and the economic crisis. Despite the probability that he himself would again face solitary confinement or death by a firing squad, Ninoy believed that he would have to return to the Philippines.

Alert to the threat to her husband's political future if Ninoy were to return to Manila, Mrs. Marcos met Ninoy in New York to try to persuade him to join the Nacionalista Party. As an inducement, she offered him a personal loan that she would have friends manage for him as an investment fund. He refused, insisting that he wanted to revive his old Liberal Party. She then reminded him that his passport had expired, and warned him that the communists were out to kill him should he return. When she was informed in July—and again in August—that Aquino was indeed returning, she responded on both occasions by saying, "If he comes back, he will be dead." Marcos's minister of defense, Juan Ponce Enrile, also warned Ninoy that return to his homeland would mean his certain death.

Ninoy was not to be thwarted by warnings; he went ahead with his plans and prepared a statement to be made on his arrival. His words:

We can be united only if all the rights and freedoms enjoyed before September 21, 1972 are fully restored. The Filipino asks for nothing more, but will surely accept nothing less.

1. [For the settlement of my disputes with Marcos], I shall define my terms: Order my immediate execution or set me free. I was sentenced to die for allegedly being the leading communist leader. I am not a communist, never was, and never will be.
2. National reconciliation and unity can be achieved but only with justice, including justice for our Muslim and Ifugao brothers. There can be no deal with a dictator. No compromise with dictatorship.
3. In a revolution there can really be no victors, only victims. We do not have to destroy in order to build.
4. Subversion stems from economic, social, and political causes and will not be solved by purely military solutions; it can be curbed not with ever increasing repression, but with a more equitable distribution of wealth, more democracy, more freedom.
5. For the economy to get going once again, the workingman must be given his just and rightful share of his labor, and to the owners and managers must be restored the hope where there is so much uncertainty if not despair.... I return from exile and to an uncertain future with only determination and faith to offer—faith in our people and faith in God.

Clearly Ninoy felt that, whatever the cost, he had to return to the Philippines immediately. Perhaps he could effect a reconciliation with Marcos. Perhaps he could persuade Marcos to abolish the infamous presidential commitment orders (PCOs), give up the right given him by Constitutional Amendment 6 to rule by decree, grant amnesty to political prisoners, and assume leadership in a peaceful transition to democracy. In any case, Ninoy would try to coalesce the fragmented opposition and prepare for the legislative elections scheduled for May 14, 1984.

In Marcos's opinion, Ninoy was a spent politician seeking headlines and plotting a spectacular *coup de théâtre*. Nevertheless, Marcos respected him as the one Filipino besides himself of presidential cal-

The assassination of Ninoy Aquino. The body on the left is that of the "communist" who was alleged to have been Ninoy's killer.

iber. Some of Marcos's friends suggested to him that Aquino recently had been treated with extraordinary courtesy in Washington and it could be that some Americans would like to see Marcos sacrificed as another Ngo Dinh Diem, the assassinated ex-president of Vietnam. Speaking with friends on the flight to Manila, Ninoy appeared to be his lighthearted self, the perfect embodiment of *Bahala Na* (the Filipino equivalent of "What will be, will be"). As his plane neared Manila, his mood changed. He looked to God in prayer. When the plane landed, the security guards came aboard as his escort. As he started down the stairs, a voice called out in Tagalog, "Here he is, here he is; shoot him, shoot him." A single shot rang out; Ninoy fell, face down, on the tarmac. Another hail of bullets, and a second body was sprawled on the ground. A new chapter in the Philippine story was about to begin.

MURDER AND
MARTYRDOM

As the news of his assassination spread, the whole nation asked, "Who killed Ninoy, and why?" For a period of twenty-four hours a sense of anarchy prevailed throughout the Philippines. Wild rumors circulated about a military coup. When Marcos finally appeared on television, he explained that Ninoy was killed by a communist hit man who was immediately shot down by a fusillade from the Aviation Security Command. Nobody believed him. Speculation mounted. The murder must have been committed by one of the security guards themselves. But why? On whose orders? Was it done to win the approval of someone higher up—General Ver (the chief of staff), the first lady, or President Marcos himself?

Beneath the pall of gloom that hung over the nation a new spirit was taking shape. A new courage was being born. Voices heretofore fearfully hidden in the underground cried out against Marcos and his evils. Who could dare remain silent if Ninoy had given his life? At once Ninoy became a symbol of resistance and hope, of determination and faith. What Ninoy gained, Marcos lost. The picture cleared: The fanciful, glamorous portraits of Marcos all over town suddenly looked ridiculous. The man who had been regarded as a political genius was seen as aged and ailing, beleaguered and confined to the palace by his shrinking coterie of sycophants.

When Ninoy was buried, more than a million people lined the route from the church to the cemetery in an extraordinary display of grief and love. Every mourner, in identifying himself with his fallen hero, took a new pride in his country and his race. One of those mourners, Teodoro Locsin, Jr., the son of one of Ninoy's oldest family friends, describes the scene in these words:

> There was the funeral, of course, where crowds bigger than those at Gandhi's silently braved the inclement weather and stood without shoving and jostling to pay their respects to the man's widow and mother, and where the man's brother, walking at the head of the procession, struck just the right note when he told the crowd at one intersection, "They killed my brother; I will get them." As he walked here, a head taller than the people around him, he was beyond politics, addressing that emotion in us that is also beyond politics and compromise.
>
> It was well into the night when the procession reached the cemetery, its progress marked by the flickering of a thousand candles pressed into hands in the darkness by unknown hands.... The coffin was slipped into the tomb

under the imperturbable gaze of the widow and the mother. Ninoy slipped into history.

THE RISING
ANTI-MARCOS TIDE

In the days that followed, students, workers, and the urban poor in Manila were joined by housewives, priests, nuns, businessmen, and clerks and secretaries in massive anti-Marcos demonstrations that lasted far into the night. Emotions ran high. One had to be in their midst to realize what they were trying to do. They were not out to overthrow the government. They demanded "Justice for Aquino, Justice for all!" They wanted an end to tyranny; they longed for the return of freedom.

Street demonstrations were more often like fiestas or carnivals than revolutionary protests. The marchers would dance and chant or shout such slogans as "Down with the U.S.-Marcos dictatorship!" It was not just the communists who expressed their bitterness over American support for the hated Marcos regime. Parades with multicolored banners and grotesque figures would often wind up with the burning of effigies of Marcos or Uncle Sam in front of the American Embassy or Malacanang. Inevitably, the carnival spirit ebbed, but the demonstrations continued. Marcos abandoned his policy of maximum tolerance as he lost patience with the demonstrators. The risk of bloodshed became apparent in every encounter between the police and the crowds. On September 21, a mere month after Ninoy's assassination, eleven youths were beaten to death in a demonstration at the Mendiola Bridge, just outside the presidential palace.

But something of profound importance was happening. The Philippine crowds in almost daily demonstrations passionately displayed their faith, determination, and courage. Filipinos had been pushed as far as they would go. To become effective against Marcos, they needed unity and they needed leadership. And a new leadership, about to emerge, took shape around the name of the martyred Aquino. Ninoy's widow and his brothers stood beside grizzled veterans in defying the club-wielding, gun-toting riot police with their water cannons and canisters of tear gas.

Already "the parliament of the streets," as the demonstrations were dubbed, began to make the Philippine story a prime-time happening in the media of the world. Meanwhile, in Manila, public sentiment against Marcos piled up like a tropical storm cloud as the president failed to take decisive steps to bring Ninoy's murderers to justice. Some of Marcos's closest friends and associates, including Prime Minister Virata, the venerable General Carlos Romulo, and Foreign Minister Arturo Tolentino, felt that suspicions of government complicity were so well-founded that without an investigation confidence in the Marcos regime would be totally destroyed.

Ninoy's widow had no doubt that Marcos himself was ultimately responsible, but she did not believe that justice could be done before Marcos was removed from office. The assassination itself had moved the hierarchy of the Roman Catholic Church under Cardinal Sin to call for a thorough and impartial public investigation. Even more significantly, it spurred the Catholic Bishops Conference of the Philippines (CBCP) to dispatch a pastoral letter to be read on Sunday in every church throughout the islands urging Marcos to put an end to his repressive decrees that violated human rights.

Marcos persisted in denying any knowledge of a conspiracy to kill Ninoy, sticking to his story that a communist hit man was the guilty party and that he had complete faith in the innocence of General Ver. Mrs. Marcos indignantly denied that she had anything to do with the murder. One afternoon in Malacañang as she was showing me the Santo Nino over the doorway, she said, "Look at the crucifix on the wrist of the statue—that was Ninoy's gift to me for all that I had done for him before he left for the States. How could I be involved?"

The handling of the Aquino case was, for Marcos, a grave mistake. In his effort to perpetuate his place at the controls of the Philippine government, he originally appointed an investigating commission that was too patently a whitewash body for the public to accept. On the second go, October 21, 1983, he appointed a five-member board under former Court of Appeals Justice Corazon Agrava to determine the facts and circumstances surrounding the Aquino killing and to "investigate all the aspects of the said tragedy." The board members were all respected persons, but no one believed that they would dare to come up with a verdict unfavorable to the president. The talk in the coffee shops in Manila was, "Why hold hearings when everybody but the board itself knows where the guilt lies?"

As the anti-Marcos tide rose, the failing economy speeded the Philippines on its downward course. Not only in Manila, but throughout the archipelago, the economy was dead in its tracks. Hunger stalked a country that had no excuse to let its people, any of them, go hungry. Food was scarce and expensive and steadily becoming more so. As workers were laid off or fired, more strikes and further labor unrest were inevitable. As production declined, trade stagnated. Soon after the Aquino assassination the Philippines was compelled to default on its foreign debts. To all intents and purposes, the country was broke.

Recovery depended on Marcos and his technocrats, and they were bankrupt in ideas, in credibility, and in public funds. Even his cronies failed him. Their enterprises went bankrupt, and the banks foreclosed—thus becoming the legal owners of worthless corporations. Private businessmen in their frustration were increasingly turning against the government. In a face-to-face meeting with representative business leaders, Marcos was bluntly told, "Mr. President, you have been in office eighteen years and that is long enough."

The Aquino assassination also caused the U.S. government to reappraise the policies that it had pursued to help the Philippines. The article of faith in Washington that the future belonged either to Marcos or to the communists no longer seemed valid, although some stubbornly clung to the belief that he could be persuaded to reform. The United States had been extending aid to Marcos because he was the government, and American aid programs had to be administered through him—no questions asked. But it was becoming increasingly clear that Marcos was not interested in democracy or reform. Aid intended to promote the common interests of the United States and the Philippines was not bringing success against communist insurgents nor was it adding to the security of American military facilities in the Philippines. It was not serving to strengthen democracy within the Philippines and was not winning for the United States any new friends among the Filipinos. It was time for a change.

American public opinion began to turn against Marcos as the great hope for stability and peace in Southeast Asia. Stories in the American press revealed the extensive financial interests outside the Philippines of Marcos, his family, and his favorites. Even the reputed military heroics of his wartime guerrilla days were being openly questioned. Policy statements from Washington indicated a cooling-off toward Marcos, but never a lack of interest or goodwill toward the Philippines. Washington repeatedly called on Marcos to hold free, fair, and honest elections for the National Assembly in the spring of 1984. Sensing that Americans (with the possible exception of President Reagan) were turning against him, Marcos said, "The Americans treat me as though I am guilty before I am tried."

In the United States attention began to shift toward the moderate opposition. The lingering fear in the United States was that the opposition—the opponents of President Marcos—were too far to the left, too close to the communists, and too closely identified with all the evils of pre-Marcos Philippine democracy. A newfound hope was that the moderates would constitute a new wave, independent of communism on the left or constitutional authoritarianism on the right. If a new vigor, a new spirit, could be found in the Philippines, and if all the fragmented, disunited, quarreling, anti-Marcos factions could only get their act together, a new leadership might emerge with which the United States could more effectively cooperate.

Seeds of opposition had been detected in the Philippines when the elections for the Interim National Assembly were permitted in 1978. Underground leaflets were circulated and effective "noise campaigns" (make a noise if you are against Marcos) or "light-a-fire protests" (light a candle if you are against Marcos) made their appearance. But the largesse of Marcos and the harshness of restrictive measures of martial law prevented the growth of any significant opposition movement. In a rigged election in 1981, he was given a near unanimous victory for another six-year term as president. Unable to ignore the rising criticism of his high-handedness, in January 1984 he put through a constitutional amendment providing new rules of succession and reestablishing the position of vice-president, to be effective in 1987.

AN ILLUSION
OF DEMOCRACY

Marcos went ahead with his plans for the National Assembly elections of May 14, 1984. Confident of victory, he relaxed the electoral ground rules to give the opposition a "sporting chance." He liberalized the rules on free speech and freedom of the press but kept control of TV and radio. He suspended the hated Preventive Detention Action (PDA) decrees which had replaced the Presidential Commitment Orders (PCOs) as the instruments of arbitrary arrest for the duration of the forty-five-day campaign. He ordered his own handpicked Committee on Elections (COMELEC) to draw up new registration lists and to take all necessary steps to prevent irregularities. The rules looked fine on the surface, but in the moment of truth they were blithely ignored.

The communists boycotted the election, as did the noncommunist, leftist-oriented diehards who felt that the whole election process was futile. They were convinced that Marcos would cheat, so that anybody who ran for office—or even voted—would be participating in a patent fraud. Three opposition groups who agreed to take part in the election served notice that they would have to be reckoned with in the future because of their incredible showing. The first was the National Democratic Front (NDF), identified with the communists and assorted "left-wing" causes; the second was the Philippine Democratic Party-Laban (Labas Ng Bayan) shortened to PDP-Laban—with Laban meaning "fight"—comprised of Aquino supporters, many of whom were former Liberals; and the third was the United National Democratic Organization (UNIDO), a nationwide party consisting mainly of ex-Nacionalistas headed by Salvador (Doy) Laurel.

The campaign was complete with entertainers, movie stars, and envelopes stuffed with pesos. Marcos and his political machine, the KBL, anticipated an easy victory, but for the first time in fifteen years the election was a horse race—despite the fragmentation of the opposition. The president himself formulated his party's program and determined its strategy. The first lady acted as the national campaign manager. She distributed the T-shirts, shopping bags, sandwiches, fruit juice, and payoffs that were needed to bring out the crowds. To her workers she said, "To win it takes plenty of this [making a circle of her thumb and forefinger to symbolize "money"], and this [pointing to her head], and this [clenching her fist for "fight"]." To one observer, Steve Lohr of the *New York Times*, she frankly said, "Campaigning costs money. Don't kid me that you can get a million people at a rally without paying. I give money to the artists who sing. I give money to pay for sandwiches. I give them everything and still I cannot be sure of their votes."

During the campaign the government drew some 5 billion pesos (U.S. $357 million) from the Central Bank to give to their local supporters. In return, the KBL (*Kilusang Bagong Lipunan*, or "New Society Movement") expected the barangay captains, the bureaucrats, and the heads of government-financed industries and banks to deliver the votes. The party platform covered all the good things, including nationalism, unity, democracy, and social justice, but the candidates and their speeches made little difference. The sole issue was: Would the president and the first lady maintain their power?

The greatest strength of the KBL lay in the weakness of the opposition, whose elements had nothing in common except their determination to get rid of Marcos. In Marcos's eyes, the opposition was "nothing but a bunch of political rejects from the old order who do nothing but besmirch the image of the country and the people." In his campaign speeches, Marcos defended his record in saving the country from the communists. He declared he used every single dollar of foreign aid and foreign loans to shore up the standard of living. He blamed the country's economic mess on the world recession, the rising price of petroleum, and the heartlessness of his creditors. He boasted of his accomplishments in land reform, food production, industrial development, public works, and welfare for the masses. In reply, the opposition said, "You have created a system of one-man rule that is not only virtually uncontrolled, but is in fact aided and abetted by a legislature which is useless, a judiciary which is subservient, a military that has been perverted, a press that is intimidated, and a Central Bank that does not know how to count."

The election itself was an old-time fiesta of bread and circuses, with the accustomed amount of fraud and violence. But the people loved it. Merely to cast their votes was another exercise in freedom. Kids played in the schoolyards around the polling booths while the old folks clustered about and argued politics. The Marcos-appointed COMELEC was said to have conducted "clean, fair, and honest" elections, but the real efforts to prevent fraud were made by 200,000 volunteers from some eighty civic organizations who, with the support of the Catholic Church, signed up with the reincarnated National Movement for Free Elections (NAMFREL) to watch the polls.

The election results produced a sense of satisfaction for everyone. Marcos, not surprisingly, won, but in spite of all the cheating his opponents captured 59 of the 183 seats. In Manila, where he thought he was strongest and where his wife was most active, he won only 6 of the 21 seats he expected to carry unanimously. This was not enough to challenge his control of the legislature, but it was more than enough to make his job more difficult. The Marcos boast that the opposition was irrelevant had been totally disproved. Marcos said, "We have presented the world an image of a free democracy." Proud of his victory, he felt that despite his illness he was at the height of his career. He professed to be good for another ten years and told his television audience that of course he would run again in 1987.

The first lady was distressed that the KBL had failed to sweep Manila; she had no idea that so many people would vote against her. But she had no intention of resigning any of her posts. She would work harder to revamp her party that had become fat, lazy, and overconfident; she would recruit new talent for her projects in Metro Manila and the Ministry of Human Settlements. The rank and file of the KBL were not so confident. Uneasy about the state of the president's health, they doubted his continuing capacity to lead. Although they speculated about a possible successor, they knew that without Marcos at the helm, the KBL would fall apart. The unity of the party was seen as directly proportionate to the strength left in the president's body.

For the moderate opposition, the strong showing at the polls on May 14 was encouraging. The winners among them would get the chance to speak out in the National Assembly; the losers would carry on the fight against Marcos in the upcoming elections for local officials. As a group, they gained immensely in credibility and legitimacy. Middle-class professionals, the "non-crony" business elite, and militant housewives in great numbers joined their ranks. Their quest for party unity led them to bury their personal quarrels and differences of opinion. Such issues as the American bases, the treatment of communists, and taking to the streets in public protests were set aside in order to accomplish their overriding aim of getting rid of Marcos—by peaceful means if possible. Their determination, singleness of purpose, and obvious integrity encouraged the Catholic hierarchy, from Cardinal Sin and the majority of the bishops down, to go all out on their behalf.

The communists did not like the moderate opposition any more than they liked Marcos, but they felt that they had gained time. They reasoned that since Marcos was the worst of the capitalist lot, and the most favored by the United States, his continuation in office would make it easier to win the eventual victory of their revolution. But whether under Marcos or under the opposition, they would continue their fight. They were not eager for power before they were in a position to handle it.

THE UNRAVELING
DICTATORSHIP

The year and a half immediately preceding the Marcos exodus from the Philippines must have been very painful indeed for him and for his entourage. His health was problematic, but he was not willing to come clean with the public and confess openly whether his physical problems were due to shrapnel in his body, lupus erythematosis, failing kidneys, or asthma. The man who had loved to box, play golf, and water ski found it difficult to move, or even to catch his breath. Some days he was up, some down. Sometimes his interviewers described him as strong and alert; at other times his appearances on television showed him to be straining for strength and the posture of command. He ventured less and less outside Malacañang—which in the Manila rumor-mill was tantamount to living on borrowed time.

The announcement by the Agrava Board of Inquiry of its findings on the Aquino assassination in October 1984 did not add to the president's state of health or peace of mind. All five board members, after a year of hearings, repudiated the military's version of the communist hit man and concluded that a conspiracy existed within the military itself. The board was divided over the level of responsibility within the military. Chairman Agrava issued a minority report naming only the chief of the Aviation Security Command, Brigadier General Luther Custodio, and six enlisted men who escorted Aquino from the aircraft, as definitely involved. The report of the other four board members implicated one civilian and twenty-five military men, including Chief of Staff General Ver. President Marcos had no choice but to put General Ver on leave-of-absence status and order the case submitted for investigation and immediate trial before a special court.

Although convinced that Marcos would manage somehow to exculpate at least General Ver, the public was not prepared to dismiss the Aquino case from its conscience. Increasingly the name Aquino gave new life to the waning spirit of the parliament of the streets. Again it was feared that the Filipino spirit would flash and then fade away. "I told you so" was the most frequent, disconsolate phrase one heard in December 1985, when the special court acquitted all 26 defendants and General Ver was ordered back to active duty. But the court's decision did nothing to change public opinion. The verdict was looked upon with indignation as a mockery of justice; it tore the last shred of respectability from the Marcos version of the traditionally independent judicial system.

Economically, the Philippines in the last days of Marcos went from bad to worse. During his last two years, real per capita income fell 17 percent, setting the economy back to where it had been a decade before. In the Philippines, with the worst pattern of income distribution in Southeast Asia, three-quarters of the population described themselves as poor. Hunger came too soon after the harvest in most provinces, and unemployment figures soared. The technocrats still could find no remedy for the mounting domestic economic ills or for the payment of foreign debts. The Philippines earned its doleful description as an economic basket case. Worst of all, even the universally respected General Romulo, who once had referred to Marcos as the "quintessential Filipino," complained to a visitor that "he [Marcos] is robbing us blind."

When Admiral William Crowe, commander-in-chief of the U.S. Pacific Command, warned the U.S. government that the Philippines had become the most dangerous, unsettling, and devastating problem on the entire Pacific Rim, American policymakers had to step up their efforts to distance themselves from President Marcos. The puzzle persisted: How to jettison Marcos without damaging the security of the Philippines? Marcos was the problem, but he was also part of the solution. A stream of visitors from the Pentagon, the State Department, the Congress, and the White House visited Manila to reason with Marcos, but he saw no need for reform. Confident in his own ability to command the Filipinos, he dismissed all his opponents as communists and all the criticisms of him as scurrilous lies invented by the liberal Western press.

He insisted that his health was unimpaired ("I can go four rounds with any of you") and that General Ver was essential for the future of the Philippine armed forces. On one occasion he said to me, "I cannot understand how naive, impertinent young whippersnappers from the Pentagon can presume to tell me how to 'reform' my armed forces when I have been in total command of these islands for nineteen years." And again he said, "I cannot understand your desire to have me put General Ramos in command of the armed forces. I know him. I helped to pay for his expenses at West Point. And I know that it was under his command that the Philippine Constabulary plummeted to the depths of dishonor and disgrace."

In his evaluation of the performance of the armed forces and the success, or lack thereof, in the war against the communist insurgents, Marcos differed with Defense Minister Enrile. Enrile paid serious attention to the complaints about the venality of the higher-ups in the military establishment, about the frustrations of the middle-level officers (many of whom had been trained in the United States), and about the hardships encountered by the common soldiers in combat zones, as well as the atrocities committed by them. Enrile was fully aware of the seriousness of the Reform the Armed Forces Movement (RAM) and the organization known as "We Belong." Marcos dismissed the need for reform, commenting that dissatisfied soldiers always complain. Enrile warned that the New People's Army (NPA) had grown to a strength of 16,000 guerrillas, supported by a million sympathizers operating in sixty-two of the country's seventy-three provinces. Marcos retorted that he could bring the NPA under control in three or four years—the same amount of time, U.S. military officials warned the Congress, that the NPA could fight the entire Philippine armed forces to a stalemate.

Clearly, the famed Marcos ability to work his political will was eroding. His own daughter, Imee, told him, "Inside Malacañang it's a snakepit, and it's chaos out there." Some of his most trusted lieutenants (Juan Ponce Enrile, Blas Ople, Adrian Cristobal) made it known that they would be available for leadership of the KBL should anything happen to Marcos. Intra-party scrambles for power became more frequent and more intense among the barangay captains, the mayors, and the governors. More individuals defected from the KBL to the opposition. Not many had faith in the ability of Marcos to revive his dying regime, and precious few would believe any public statements that he might make.

The Marcos regime was shot through with favoritism and corruption, but neither corruption nor repression could hide incompetence. The slow but steady resurgence of violence on the part of the armed forces, their killings, torture, and arbitrary imprisonment, made the country—as Bishop Fortich of Negros described it—a social volcano about to explode.

2

"Get me a million signatures
on a petition and I'll run."

Cory Aquino

THE PEOPLE'S REVOLUTION

In late November 1985, Marcos decided he would bite the bullet. It was on David Brinkley's national television show that he was goaded into declaring that he would call a snap election for the presidency early in 1986 and once and for all settle what he characterized as the "childish claims" about his popularity. Confident that neither ballots nor bullets could remove him from office, he told his people in Manila that they could inform the opposition that he would see them at their funerals. Relying on his own charisma, his formidable wife, the technocrats and bureaucrats dependent on him, the army, his cronies, and the public purse, he anticipated victory as usual. He was in for a tremendous surprise. The revolution, as everybody in Manila calls it, was about to happen.

CORY VERSUS MARCOS

Most unexpectedly, the opposition closed ranks. The communists refused to cooperate, but, thanks largely to the untiring efforts of Cardinal Sin, the bulk of the anti-Marcos forces united to support Cory Aquino for president and Doy Laurel for vice-president. Cory was a genuinely reluctant candidate, but, as she confided to friends, "I made a pledge to my husband when I kissed him in his coffin, that I would continue his fight for the cause of justice and democracy." She turned to the venerable publisher, "Chino" Roces, and told him, "Get me a million signatures on a petition and I'll run."

The 53-year-old housewife, who Imelda said was "not pretty enough to be smart," ran a campaign that was a political miracle. Without experience, she handled crowds with ease and grace that would have done justice to Franklin Roosevelt or Ronald Reagan. I saw her stir the emotions of Filipinos as I had seen Quezon and Magsaysay do before her. And she did it without gimmicks, bribes, or promises. Her appeal was her integrity, her strength of character, and her charisma. As one observer said, "You may not agree with her program, but you can almost smell the honesty."

Her closest friends—her relatives, priests from the Ateneo University, a handful of businessmen, lawyers, professors, journalists, and one lone public relations counselor—ran her campaign. Her downtown headquarters was bedlam, bustling with more photographers and media types in search of news than campaign workers. No organization, no funds—only a reincarnation of the faith and determination that had inspired Ninoy. "Mr. Marcos is determined to remain permanent dictator, come hell or high water," she said. "I am determined to stop him."

On the campaign trail, Cory learned the profound meaning of "People Power." No television, scarcely any radio coverage, no claques. She relied on the yellow ribbons, the yellow T-shirts, and the yellow dresses to whip up enthusiasm. She spurned security. The women and children walking with her, or surrounding her car, gave her better protection against the goons than any armed escort could have provided. In listening to the voices of the multitudes in Mindanao, in Cebu, as well as in Manila, the realization deepened within her that she really was the people's choice, the one to whom they looked for a better future. Her personal life became secondary; her total commitment was to her country. When someone suggested that without security she might be killed, she simply responded, "It does not matter; I'll be with Ninoy sooner."

According to Cory, the real issue was the performance of Marcos:

> How he and his cronies plundered the economy and mortgaged our future;

How he and his dummies have drained the National Treasury and stashed their hidden wealth abroad;

How he and his goons have tortured and "salvaged" defenseless citizens;

How he and his political padrinos have turned the *Batasan* (National Assembly) into an expensive rubber stamp;

How he and his misguided minions have prostituted professionalism in the military;

And how he and his classmates have converted the Supreme Court into a compliant cabal of callous collaborators.

Her speeches were primarily anti-Marcos, and she attacked him with no holds barred:

I am here in Mindanao in the midst of the violence and devastation Marcos has wrought. And I am not afraid to be here. But Mr. Marcos is.

I accuse Mr. Marcos of cowardice because he will not come to Mindanao to stand in the physical presence of the people he has hurt and betrayed.

I accuse Mr. Marcos of cowardice because he will not stand before me and dare to hurl his charges in my face and let my answers be heard.

I accuse Mr. Marcos of cowardice because he needed over 2,000 troops to kill one man—Ninoy Aquino. And he has the gall to say he fought off hordes of Japanese soldiers at Besang Pass. What a laugh!

I accuse Mr. Marcos of cowardice because he whimpers about a little scratch on his hand and ignores the hole that his people blew out of the face of Jeremiah de Jesus and the mangled bodies of the opposition after the grenade attack he launched at them in Plaza Miranda.

I accuse Mr. Marcos of trying to cover up his cowardice with a salad of military decorations, none of which he ever earned in the field of honor.

I challenge Mr. Marcos to stand up, like a woman, and answer my charges of his cowardice with truth—if he dares.

In her speeches before serious, specialized audiences, she was no-nonsense, low-key, slyly humorous, humble, and honest. At a meeting at the Intercontinental Hotel, I found it impossible to get near the podium. Three thousand people listened to loudspeakers outside a room that could seat only 400. She spoke simply and in parables, as she had learned to do in her younger days. Her theme: "Oh, Pharaoh, let my people go; let the Filipino people go." Almost every sentence won applause. Chants of "Coree! Coree!" made it next to impossible for her to get on with her speech. And when she left the hotel, it was like the captain of the football team pushing his way through the student crush after winning the big game.

A few paragraphs reveal the fervor of Cory's attack on Marcos:

> As I stand to face this international gathering, I feel in my heart a deep pain.
>
> I feel pain and also shame.
>
> I think of our highest monetary officials compelled to swallow their pride in international negotiations: Mr. Virata and Mr. Fernandez knocking humbly at every banker's door and offering profuse thanks, even for loans grudgingly given and on humiliating terms to a government that cannot be trusted.
>
> I think of Prime Minister Lee Kuan Yew, proud leader of a city state one-fourth the size of Metro Manila, publicly doubting the capacity of our nation of 50 million people to show the fortitude needed to rise to the challenge of shared responsibility in the ASEAN community.
>
> I think of Congressman Solarz pointing an accusing finger at Mr. Marcos and his first lady for stealing pesos and centavos from our countless poor to stash them away in the form of multi-million-dollar real estate holdings abroad while our children starve and millions are unemployed.
>
> I think of our highest military officers forced to answer embarrassing questions from American investigators digging into shady transactions in the disposition of foreign aid.
>
> I think of Senator Paul Laxalt, grey-haired like a Grecian oracle, solemnly secretive of the burden of his message from Mr. Reagan but broadly hinting that Mr. Marcos must end

his wanton ways lest he plunge the nation further towards irreversible disaster.

Finally, I think of sensitive official documents from United States military archives, declassified at last after forty years, unraveling a sordid story of fraud and fantasy upon which Mr. Marcos has anchored his political career, a career which I have vowed to end.

And now hundreds of foreign correspondents and observers have swarmed to our land, curious to see whether this nation, gripped in a crisis of cruelty and corruption, can redeem itself.

I have reflected and I have asked myself: What is it that has brought this nation to its knees? Who has brought us this posture of humiliation and ridicule before the world? Who has desecrated the Pearl of the Orient?

The answer is inescapably clear—Mr. Marcos. The same Mr. Marcos who, even in the years when the idealism of youth should have ennobled his soul, did not hesitate to fabricate fantastic feats of heroism for a measly measure of military back-pay and a spurious salad of mythical medals.

As he began his public life, so he is ending it.

He dragged us to the pit where we are today through a policy of mendacity and deceit. The conduct of his current political campaign—by lies, by smears, by half-truths and fairy tales woven out of thin air—is a shameless proclamation that there is not one iota of remorse in his soul.

And so I say to Mr. Marcos what Moses said to the cruel, enslaving Pharaoh—Let our people go! Let the Filipino people go! *Tama na! Sobra na! Palitan na!* [Enough, too much; it's time for a change.]

The grand climax of Cory's campaign came with the final rally at the Luneta. Cory supporters walked for miles to get there, dancing, singing, and waving their yellow banners and streamers along the way. A half-million people jammed the park. "My God," my companion said, "I have never seen so many people, let alone been in the middle of them." The words of the speakers, Cory and Doy, did not matter. The listeners wanted to scream, to explode—which they did—until near-exhaustion drove them home. On the rooftop of the neighboring Manila Hotel, ABC, CBS, and NBC caught the whole scene and sent it by satellite to every home in the United States.

THE MARCOS
THREE-RING CAMPAIGN

What a contrast to the campaign of President Marcos and his running mate, Arturo Tolentino, which I followed with as much diligence as I did that of the opposition! The Marcos colors of red, white, and blue replaced Cory's yellow. The Marcos machine was well-oiled and professionally conducted. The television, radio, and press constantly extolled his achievements and carried such welcome announcements as a reduction in the gasoline tax, a 10 percent pay hike, and cost-of-living bonuses for all government employees (including the military) effective January 1.

Marcos conducted himself like a king—above it all, disdaining the hoopla of the noisy opposition. In his speeches he ducked substantive issues and showed no interest in reforms that might be expected if he were reelected. Facetiously, he asked, "What nincompoop will Cory get to run her government?" He attacked Cory as being soft on communism and anti-American. "You have had no experience," he charged. "That's right," she replied, "I have no experience in the killings, the corruption, and the favoritism that has brought this country into the abyss." Marcos made a serious mistake when he remarked, "A woman's place is in the bedroom," and Mrs. Marcos did not help their cause when she said, "Imagine the audacity of Mrs. Aquino thinking she could run the country. Imagine—a housewife."

Two days after Cory's speech at the Intercontinental, Marcos was guest of honor at the same hotel. This time I had no trouble getting a seat up front. In the midst of his uninspiring remarks, Marcos made a flamboyant gesture of signing into law a number of decrees intended to bring joy to the business community. His speech fell flat. The fire had gone from the old Marcos in spite of a painful effort to marshal his strength for one last victory. The next day an editorial commented, "His voice has lost its command. He is an emperor walking naked, clothed only by praises and paeans from supporters who are themselves garbed in robes snatched from the country's starving and dying population."

At the climactic Marcos rally in Luneta Park on the day following the Cory rally, the celebrants did not walk; they rode to the park in public buses paid for from public funds. The Marcos crowd was a sea of red, white, and blue, but it lacked the Cory enthusiasm. This was not a cross-section of ordinary citizens, but a gathering of the pitiful and the proud who had come to rely on the favor of Malacañang. The food was free, and so was the entertainment provided by the best comedians, singers, and movie stars. My room-boy at the hotel was also at the Marcos rally and I asked him how he liked it. "It was all right," he said. "My boss [Roberto Benedicto, the owner of the hotel and one of Marcos's favorite cronies] gave me 500 pesos to attend, but I am still going to vote for Cory."

The carnival atmosphere of the campaign could not dispel a dark foreboding that something terrible might happen before the election was finished. A Filipino friend sent his wife and grandson to Hong Kong because of his fear of a military coup. Marcos warned that if there were violence, he would not hesitate to crush it. Cory's people firmly stated that even if Cory lost, the revolution would go on: "We will boycott the crony businesses, such as San Miguel; we will cause work slowdowns, noise barrages, and a general strike; come April 15, we will refuse to pay our taxes." In their view they were in the midst of a revolution, and a revolution is not an embroidery party.

As election day neared, the Catholic bishops circulated another pastoral letter admonishing the voters to "Vote, vote well. Make sure the election is honest and free. Take the money if you must, and then vote for your own choice. Remember that no one is obliged to fulfill an evil contract."

On the big day itself, February 7, 1986, my companion and I first visited an ordinary polling place where nothing seemed amiss. The scene was the usual one of laughing, playing children, and the older folks vehemently but good-naturedly arguing the merits of their respective candidates. It came to our attention very soon, however, that something novel was occurring in the way of cheating. A goodly number of people could not vote because their names could not be found on the voting register! It was later learned that a computerized scam all over the country had neatly removed the names of Cory supporters. This tactic alone may have resulted in the disfranchisement of up to six million voters.

Volunteer poll-watchers (NAMFREL) had been briefed to cope with fake ballots, flying voters (voters who flit from precinct to precinct, voting at each stop), and ballot-box stuffing, but they were not prepared either for the tampering with the voting register or the eventual manipulation of the vote-counting process. One bank of computers at NAMFREL headquarters operated under the eye of Cory partisans; a second bank at the Commission on Election (COMELEC) headquarters was Marcos-controlled. The only official count, however, was to be one independently conducted and certified by the National Assembly, the Marcos rubber stamp. Many oldtimers were of the opinion that all nominal safeguards for a free, fair, and honest election were completely irrelevant. By controlling the final count, Marcos would proclaim his victory by whatever margin he desired.

The counting process took days. The early returns from Metro Manila gave Cory a substantial lead. As later returns from the provinces came trickling in, the COMELEC count showed Marcos forging slowly ahead. The trend inevitably indicated a Marcos victory. But three days into the counting process, thirty COMELEC computer operators walked away from their jobs in protest against the fraudulent count for which they felt responsible. The COMELEC count was suspended. Fully aware of the massive manipulation taking place, Cory issued a public statement. "To Mr. Marcos I say, with much sacrifice and suffering, the people have given me their mandate. I shall protect it with my life."

"I WILL NOT BE CHEATED OUT OF MY VICTORY"

Although the election was over, Manila was in the grip of uncertainty and fear. What was going to happen? No matter what the NAMFREL count would ultimately show, the Cory total would be shy the missing millions of votes. In any free, fair, and honest reckoning of the election results, Cory was far and away the winner. But Marcos was in the driver's seat. He flooded the media with his allegation that it was not he, but the Cory side, that had done the cheating. He let the National Assembly's count continue. It was expected that in its own good time the Assembly would ceremoniously announce the Marcos victory. As the climax of the scenario, the president would have himself proclaimed for another term.

Many on the Marcos team were disgusted with the whole election procedure and felt despondent about the future. One of his closest advisers told him directly, "Mr. President, it would have been better if you had lost." Another remarked in private, "There is nothing left; there is no way that he can make the reforms we so desperately need." A third, one of his closest intimates in Malacanang, said, "When the history of the Philippines is written, it will contain just two lines on

Marcos: (1) He was the man who imposed martial law, illegally and in the absence of any communist threat, and (2) that everything he did afterwards was a failure, specifically the New Society." Even in the face of the mandate that he was supposed to have received from the voters, the old team had no appetite to undertake what they considered a hopeless job.

Cory was fighting mad. She felt that she had won and she declared "I will not be cheated out of my victory." Buoyed by the rising tide of People Power, she would not publicly accede defeat. Cardinal Sin and the bishops backed her to the limit, providing her with ample spiritual support for subsequent civil disobedience. They still stood for national reconciliation, but not at the cost of selling out to Marcos. Direct and tearful pleading by the first lady could not deter the Bishops' Conference from issuing a pastoral letter blasting Marcos's performance and telling the people it would not be a sin to disobey him. The country moved ever closer to the brink of anarchy or civil war.

As the Philippine story developed, the Americans became increasingly involved. Senator Richard Lugar, chairman of the U.S. Senate Foreign Relations Committee, headed a team of official observers sent to monitor the election and to report their findings to President Reagan. Cautious at first, the observers reported that there might have been cheating on both sides. Reagan called on *both* sides to compromise, thus infuriating the Aquino forces. As further evidence of overwhelming cheating on Marcos's part reached the White House, Reagan issued a follow-up statement blasting only the ruling party. He sent Ambassador Philip Habib as his personal envoy to assess the desires and needs of the Filipino people and to help advise him on how the United States could best pursue the goals of nurturing democracy and instituting reforms in the Philippines.

Habib arrived in Manila just when the dispute over who won seemed insoluble and the danger of bloodshed was greatest. Three elements in the situation were crystal clear: Marcos was finished; Cory was a genuine leader; and the ballgame was far from over. Marcos was, of course, ready and willing to receive Habib, but neither Cory nor Laurel, her running mate, was disposed to meet with him. Bearing in mind Habib's conciliatory role in Lebanon, they feared he had been sent to Manila to persuade them to accept a Marcos victory and to "kiss and make up." Realizing, however, that it would be foolish for them to turn their backs on the representative of the President of the United States, they agreed to meet with Habib and explain to him their side of what they saw as the fight between Marcos and the Philippine people.

Meanwhile, Marcos and the first lady got no sympathy from the American media. They were lampooned in news stories and savaged on television. Stories of their ill-gotten wealth and investments abroad won a Pulitzer prize for writers on the *San Jose Mercury News*. The man in the street was far more determined than the government in its belief that Marcos must go.

It was still Washington's official line to be patient, to avoid hasty over-interference in Philippine affairs, and to insist that whatever had to be done to bring about a change in Manila would have to be done by the Filipinos themselves. A resolution condemning Marcos passed the U.S. Senate by a near-unanimous vote, and a House Committee began hearings looking into the Marcos investments. Suggestions were made that further economic and military aid should be curtailed or suspended as long as Marcos was in power or until reforms were accomplished.

MANILA'S FOUR
MIRACLE DAYS

The Filipinos rose to the occasion, and their own courage—abetted by Marcos's mistakes—brought about the most spectacular non-violent revolution the world has ever seen. For twenty-one years Marcos, now sixty-eight, had personified power. Yet in four short days the heart of Philippine society, from the militia to the masses, turned swiftly and nearly bloodlessly against him. Marcos himself could not believe how the mighty had fallen. Neither could the crowds who toppled him, nor the millions of people around the world who watched—live and in color—a revolution where crowds were singing, tanks were stopped dead in their tracks by nuns and housewives, and people protected the armed forces rather than the other way around. As Cardinal Sin expressed it, "The force of the Filipino people stormed heaven with prayer and God answered with a miracle."

Believing that the Reform of the Armed Forces Movement (RAM) had become sufficiently strong to threaten his rule, Marcos ordered the arrest of his own minister of defense, Juan Ponce Enrile, and the acting chief of staff, Lieutenant General Fidel V. Ramos, together with opposition leaders in the Assembly and Cory's key advisers. Enrile, it is to be remembered, is the Harvard educated lawyer turned soldier, architect of the martial law structure and loyal supporter of Marcos during his entire administration. Ramos, a cousin of President Marcos and also an Ilocano, is a West Point graduate, the highly respected hope for military reform—as opposed to General Ver, the Marcos favorite, who was generally regarded as the symbol of all that needed reform in the armed forces.

On the afternoon of Saturday, February 22, 1986, Enrile decided the time had come to carry out his plot to overthrow the Marcos regime. In his office at military headquarters he was assured by Ramos, "I'll be with you all the way." Enrile telephoned Cardinal Sin and the American and Japanese ambassadors, saying very simply, "We have been discovered, they are coming to arrest me." Then he called a press conference, complete with camera crews, to inform the media of the Philippines and the world that he and Ramos had broken ranks and demanded that the president resign. To the press, he unburdened his soul for two hours. He told how Marcos, with the help of such as himself, had stolen the elections, and admitted that he personally had helped add thousands of ballots to the total of the Marcos vote. He even admitted that the basis for the declaration of martial law fourteen years earlier—a supposed attempt on Enrile's life—was a fraud. There had been in fact no conspiracy on the part of the communists or anyone else. This confession of his own misdeeds was enough to bar him from any future position of public trust.

While Enrile was supplying banner headlines for the evening news, Cardinal Sin took to the air over the church radio—Radio Veritas—and asked millions of people to take to the streets to protect the rebels, those brave soldiers who had joined with Enrile and Ramos. Said the Cardinal, "Let us not allow a drop of blood to be shed."

Spurning press and radio, at about 10:00 P.M. that same Saturday Marcos appeared on his own television station to announce that a coup was under way, and that a plot had been uncovered to assassinate him and the first lady. He said he had the power to liquidate the rebel leaders, but that he would rather they "stop this stupidity and surrender." Marcos's power was waning; "People Power" was about to take over. In response to the Cardinal's appeal, crowds formed a solid phalanx around the military camps where Enrile and Ramos were beleaguered. Armed with nothing more than rosaries and crucifixes, they simply lay down to sleep through the night.

Cory Aquino had no warning of the drama about to unfold in Manila. She was in Cebu, 500 miles to the south, on a swing around the islands, asking Filipinos to begin a series of nonviolent protests

Priests and nuns pray the Rosary in front of tanks manned by soldiers loyal to Gen. Fabian Ver.

aiming to disrupt, and ultimately bring down, the Marcos regime. When she heard the news of the Enrile-Ramos revolt she telephoned them, offering her prayers—which was all she could do to help.

Sunday morning the media blitz continued. The rebels said very clearly, "This is not a military coup d'etat; it is a revolution of the people. We support the Aquino government and we call on everyone who opposes Marcos to join us." Marcos repeated his appeals for surrender; he and General Ver then sent 500 marines in tanks to attack the rebels. But the streets were blocked—by stalled autos, trucks, and trailers, and broken cement blocks—and by thousands upon thousands of teenagers, college students, nuns, priests, lawyers, businessmen, and housewives, their arms linked to form a human barrier. The tanks stopped, the marines dismounted, and even took aim with their rifles. Nuns fell to their knees in prayer and young girls stepped forward offering flowers. One girl scrambled atop a tank and hung a rosary over a gun barrel. Another pounded on the closed lid. When a soldier opened the hatch, she handed him a stalk of blossoms. The tanks turned and retreated toward Malacañang. A temporary standoff, but what would the morning bring?

During the evening Enrile telephoned Ambassador Bosworth, advising him that many Americans were among the crowds and that their lives, too, were endangered. Then Enrile phoned General Ver, warning him that "You and the president will go down in history as butchers of your own people, butchers of civilians, butchers of foreign media men, unless you stop the tanks." Then Enrile said to the president, "We will accept no compromise; you must step down." Marcos replied, "Surrender, and you will be pardoned." On hearing the news in Washington at this point, White House Chief of Staff Don Regan is said to have advised, "Don't drive Marcos out"; Habib to have affirmed "the Marcos era has ended"; and the president himself to have concluded that "Marcos will be welcomed in the United States should he decide to leave."

Monday morning (Manila time) the tension grew. An irate Marcos, speaking from the palace, said that Enrile wanted power for himself. "I shall set the tanks and the artillery on him—I shall never resign or leave the country." Enrile calmly told the people outside his camp, "Never again will there be a tyrant in Malacañang." At 9:30 A.M. Marcos announced on television that the policy of maximum tolerance had ended, and he declared a state of emergency. Fighting words then gave way to military actions. Former Marcos men—fighter pilots, helicopter pilots, navy men, and units from the field—flocked to the rebel side. Rebel forces captured the nerve center of the government's communications network. General Ver ordered the tanks once again to storm the rebels' encampment. Rebel helicopters dropped grenades on Malacañang, and under escort of ex-Marcos jet-fighters attacked the government's air base near the Manila airport. At 6:00 P.M. Manila time, Monday, February 24, the White House announced that a transition of power in Manila was desirable and that attempts to prolong the life of the present regime were futile.

Within hours the legend of "People Power" was born and the Filipino people experienced their most glorious moment. Marcos, with only one TV channel remaining, still proclaimed, although his family was cowering in terror, "We have no intention of going abroad; we will defend the republic unto the last breath of our lives and to the last drop of our blood." The rebels, with their own recently secured TV channel, called on their military comrades to join them. By nightfall they had won over about 80 percent of the military.

Rolling relentlessly toward the rebel headquarters, Marcos's tanks again encountered a barricade of human flesh. "Keep smiling," a priest admonished them. "Make sure they understand they can only pass over your bodies." A nun, crucifix in hand, leaped upon the lead tank, tapped on the turret, and shouted for the captain to come out. When he and his soldiers emerged, girls and boys offered them sandwiches, soft drinks, and cigarettes. "Let's talk," said the nun, "there's no need to kill; we're all Filipinos." An instant—an eternity— of terrible tension, and then the tension snapped. The soldiers refused to fire. As the tanks turned back to base, the soldiers tossed their caps into the air. Forty thousand voices screamed into the night, "We love you, we love you." Emotions exhausted, everybody laughed through the tears streaming down their cheeks. As one young lady said, "It was wilder than New Year's. We all wanted to shout, to cheer Laban (Cory's fight theme), and to wave the "L" sign at anyone. We were unmindful of the time, the company, or the place. We were, we are, *free*."

The climax of the Philippine story was reached that Monday night in Manila, but the play had not yet ended. At 5:30 A.M. Tuesday, February 25—the blackest day (I am sure) in the life of President Marcos—he received a telephone call from Senator Paul Laxalt, saying, "I think you should cut and cut clean.... I think the time has come." Said Marcos slowly, "I am so very, very disappointed." At 9:00 A.M. he called Enrile, "I want a graceful exit. I'll cancel the elections. We'll organize a provisional government: you, me, and Cory. I'll remain president until 1987 so we can leave politics in an orderly manner."

But it was too late.

Shortly after 10:00 that Tuesday morning, without any evidence of being affected by the Marcos intrigues, and in the presence of Ninoy's mother, her own closest relatives, and both Enrile and Ramos, Cory Aquino took the oath of office as President of the Philippines. Never mind that the proceeding was slightly irregular; its legitimacy would be left to an uncertain future.

At noon the same day Marcos was inaugurated in a ceremony at Malacañang. For the moment the Philippines had two presidents but no government. In the middle of his inauguration, Marcos was knocked off Philippine television, this time permanently, as the rebels captured the last government communications outlet. From noon on Tuesday, Marcos was out of touch with the outside world, except by telephone. As his military protection, even the elite palace guard, slipped away from him he feared the rebels would bomb the palace and possibly murder him and his family. Only he knows the depth of his soul-searching before, at 5:00 A.M., he phoned a message to Enrile: "Stop your people from their firing." Then he phoned the American ambassador: "I want a military escort; I want to leave the palace." Not a word was said about destination, but Washington, the U.S. Embassy, and Cory were agreed that he would have to leave the country.

At 9:00 P.M., four U.S. helicopters took off with Marcos and his party and faded into the Manila night. Marcos later claimed that he was practically kidnapped to Hawaii when he really wanted and intended to go only to his beloved home in Ilocos Norte. This tale of alleged trickery was effectively laid to rest by Ambassador Bosworth, who said in Cebu on May 16, 1986, "I know personally that every time ex-president Marcos got on an airplane he knew where the helicopter or airplane was going. He knew the helicopter was going to Clark Field; he knew the C-141 was going to Guam and then to Hawaii. There was no attempt by anyone, particularly not by the United States, to somehow deceive him as to what his destination was."

Thus, the Marcos chapter in the Philippine story came to a sorry end. Within hours after the Marcoses' flight, the ornate rooms of the presidential palace were overrun by exuberant mobs who pried open desks, smashed family portraits, and made off with any souvenirs they could carry away. For Marcos and his cronies, it was the twilight of the gods; for Cory and her supporters, it was the opportunity to make a fresh start in improving the lives of the Philippine people.

3

"Her usurpation of the
presidency was the biggest robbery
in political history."

Former President Ferdinand Marcos

THE MARCOS LEGACY

On the morning after the departure of President Marcos and his party, no one believed that the millennium had arrived. There was only the immense feeling of relief that the people of the Philippines had narrowly escaped a bloodbath. Joy was everywhere but, as General Ramos expressed it, "The country is still deep in a big, black hole." The doom-sayers in the Philippines and in the United States still feared that the Philippines might become another Nicaragua or Iran.

It was comforting to speak of the revolution as a *fait accompli*. This was not, however, a revolution completed. It was only a beginning, an opportunity to make a fresh start toward a better future. With a new symbol emerging in the person of a courageous and inspiring woman, a fresh cleansing spirit swept over the land. Apart from President Aquino the new leaders were familiar figures in traditional Philippine politics. What had been enacted was little more than a changing of the guard. Would the new administration fulfill the people's hopes and live up to its promise, or would it succumb to the same pitfalls that had entrapped its predecessors? If a complete revolution were to occur in the Philippines it would have to come in the days ahead.

The next chapters in the Philippine story, like the previous ones, will have to be written by the Filipinos themselves. The entire nation—not the government, or President Aquino, alone—is faced with a challenge. The President has no further need to demonstrate her readiness to carry her share of the burden. The talent and resources of *all* the people will be needed to solve the problems of politics, economics, military reform, insurgencies, relations with the United States, and the resumption by the Philippines of its responsible role in the world community.

Too long the Filipinos have looked to Manila, specifically to the couple in the Malacañang palace, for the solution of their problems and the alleviation of their troubles. This ingrained habit has led to the question, "Is *she* [Cory] equal to the enormous tasks that lie ahead?" This is the wrong question. It is also pointless to ask, "Do the Filipino people have the innate qualities needed to put their house in order?" Four days in February 1986 gave ample evidence of their courage and spiritual strength. The right question to ask—the clue as to whether or not the Philippine story will move toward a happier ending—is, "Will the institutions and behavior patterns of Philippine society measure up to the tests of regeneration at home and respectability abroad?" Capabilities must be transformed into accomplishments. The spectacular moment of the overthrow of the tyrant has passed into history; the work of national rehabilitation is just beginning.

The challenge is not only to clean up the mess that Marcos left behind; it is also to eliminate the social ills that made Marcos and his one-man rule possible. A healthy society is the essential breeding ground for a successful democracy and a prosperous economy. It was fundamentally the flaws in the Philippine social fabric that gave Marcos his opportunity and that now feed the protest and insurgency movements throughout the country. In attacking social injustices, Cory must persevere where previous administrations have failed. Quirino, Magsaysay, Macapagal, and Marcos all produced blueprints for land reform and national development, but their performances fell far short of their promises. The Aquino administration is about to give it another try.

THE MARCOS
POLITICAL HERITAGE

Marcos made a mockery of democratic principles and practices. He betrayed those followers who had entrusted him with authoritarian rule. He violated his own program, which, on launching, had sounded so good. He flouted the rule of law and showed nothing but contempt for the political institutions that had been so zealously fostered.

By the end of his twenty years in office, all the ordinary standards of political morality had collapsed. The whole nation was caught up in the cynicism of "What's in it for me?" The Marcos entourage lived by the creed that wealth is power—the more wealth accumulated, the more effective the exercise of power. The lifestyles of the president, his extravagant wife, and his three grasping children were blasphemous role models for his suffering people. Examples of personal integrity in public office or unselfish devotion to the general welfare were all too rare.

How and why graft and corruption became, under Marcos, the dominant features of political life is easy to understand. Politics was still the monopoly of the elite and the articulate, but Marcos made it possible for more people and new talent to enter the game. In attempting to attract the best and brightest, he could not possibly offer decent rewards for their services within the limits of the law. How could a middle-grade army officer live on $100 per month, a bureau chief on $150, or a member of the cabinet on a mere $250, which is still the Philippine pay scale? Everyone—from the traffic cop to the overstaying generals—had to live on extortion, bribery, kickbacks, double-dipping, moonlighting, smuggling, or worse. Anyone with a job or access to influence had to take care of his relatives; patrons had to look after the best interests of their clients.

Marcos became the biggest patron of them all. He dispensed favors on a massive scale, and expected loyalty—and 10 percent—in return. The Filipino sense of obligation bound vast numbers of followers to him in a personal way. Everybody with a scheme to make money wanted him for a partner. Whenever he wanted a job to be done, he could find a hundred people willing to serve him. The Marcos connection was a guarantee of success.

His ultimate downfall was due not only to his immorality but also to his failures and his excesses. He did too much for too few and neglected or antagonized too many. As his skills and his faculties deserted him, he became more irrational and repressive. As his grand designs failed to materialize, and as his cronies let him down, he failed to perceive the disastrous consequences of the shrinkage of his own power base. In his greed, he overreached what Filipinos were willing to accept. He was completely impervious to the rising moral indignation on the part of decent citizens—particularly the youth—and he grossly underestimated the political power of the Catholic church, which understandably regarded itself as the guardian of the nation's moral welfare.

As his legacy, Marcos left the nation with its moral standards blighted and its political machinery in a shambles. The old, familiar Nacionalista and Liberal parties having been disbanded, and authoritarian rule discredited, the Filipino people found themselves fragmented into thousands of ex-KBL members looking for a new political home. A PDP-Laban-Unido coalition was flush with victory but uncertain about its ability to stick together. A plethora of cause-oriented groups were ready to die for their own pet concerns but practically disinterested in everything else, and only the communists were ready to offer a political umbrella for everything and everyone identified with anti-capitalism. The land was awash with voters seeking to attach themselves to dependable leaders and with aspiring leaders desperately seeking ways and means to put together and sustain an effective nationwide political organization.

With Marcos and his family gone, with General Ver and his three military sons under a cloud and the most illustrious of Marcos's cronies under public attack, the KBL was no more than a skeleton. From Honolulu, neither Marcos nor Imelda was willing to concede that the KBL was dead, although it was apparent that the once awesome political machine had lost its financial support, its symbolic aura, and its credibility. Marcos, however, issuing a barrage of phone messages, called for his people to fight on for "freedom and justice." He still regarded himself as the legitimate president of the Philippines. Denouncing Cory as the "real dictator and tyrant," he declared, "Her usurpation of the presidency was the biggest robbery in political history." He was convinced that in the long run the world, including the United States, would see that he was the only one that could save the Philippines from communism. Imelda, too, believed that even without her husband, her "little people" would clamor for her return.

Marcos never prepared an alternative leader to succeed him. According to Blas Ople, the former secretary of labor and one concerned with preserving the good fortunes of the KBL, "We all lived in a kind of forced mediocrity under the shade of the banyan tree. All I could do was engage him in verbal jousts, like a grain of sand that irritates the oyster, so that in the end a pearl of thought emerges." Such able cronies as Eduardo ("Danding") Cojuangco and Robert ("Bobby") Benedicto were never given a chance to demonstrate their political skills. It was perilous for anyone close to Marcos to show too much promise. His worldly-wise personal secretary, Alejandro ("Alex") Melchor, was banished from the inner circle of Malacañang when Mrs. Marcos came to believe he threatened her primacy. Doy Laurel had broken with Marcos, not because of differences in political philosophy, but because of his objections to the Marcos methods of operation. Juan Ponce Enrile, Marcos's minister of defense, said that when he closed his desk at the end of each day, he was never certain there would be a job for him tomorrow.

With Marcos gone, the *abandonados* were divided in their loyalties. True, some of his Ilocano compatriots would never turn against him; nor would many of those he had appointed to civilian and military offices. As Ople remarked, "A good many of us owe the president and the first lady a lot because they helped advance our careers in the past. They have done this for thousands who manned the KBL posts everywhere." Besides, he still had millions of pesos to spend.

As the result of Marcos's selfishness and shortsightedness, the thousands who rode comfortably on the bandwagon of the KBL found themselves leaderless, deprived of their financial patron, and without cohesion. A motley array of technocrats, governors, mayors, barangay captains, and displaced civil servants were left with no alternative but to scramble for their political lives. Far too numerous to be permanent outcasts from the political process, their future would depend upon the implementation of President Aquino's well-touted policy of reconciliation.

FRAGMENTATION
OF THE OPPOSITION

As long as Marcos was in power, he was the obvious target against whom all types of opposition could rally. In this environment, Cory was the ideal leader. But she was clearly a one-time phenomenon. She would serve the people as long as she was constitutionally obligated to. She had no interest in building up a political machine of her own and had firmly stated that under no circumstances would she ever run for office again. The PDP-Laban coalition that brought victory to Cory stood squarely for a nationalistic, pro-Catholic, and slightly left-of-center social orientation. It advocated the recognition of the communists as a legal party and stood for the ultimate removal of the American facilities on the Philippine military bases. It would accept the present agreement on the bases until its termination in 1991, after which the PDP-Laban coalition, led by Cory, would keep its options open.

The departure of Marcos was as damaging to the unity of the moderate opposition party as it was to the KBL. With their common enemy defeated, the struggle for power within the opposition began in earnest. Their differences were only partly ideological; they were primarily personal, so that, not surprisingly, the coalition was immediately threatened by internal rivalries. The PDP portion of the coalition had its roots in the south, with its destiny temporarily tied to Aquilino ("Nene") Pimentel of Mindanao. Pimentel, known as "Mr. Clean" of the PDP, had been arrested three times and held for a year in house detention during martial law. He agreed with Cory on the recognition of the communists, but he wanted the Americans out of the bases at once. A notorious headline seeker, he enjoyed the reaction to such remarks as "If Ronald Reagan can be president of the United States, any ass can be president of the Philippines." More than anything, he wanted to be president of the Philippines, but whether anyone except Cory could keep the coalition together was questionable.

The Machiavellian linkage between the PDP-Laban and Doy Laurel's UNIDO was very tenuous. Realizing that Cory's presence as number one on the anti-Marcos ticket was essential, Doy had accepted his supporting role as the nominee for vice-president with good grace. Far less bitterly anti-Marcos than Cory, he stayed in the background during the campaign while she led the attack on Marcos the man and on his record. Laurel generally agreed with Cory's stand on the communists and the bases, but he was far more tolerant than Cory of the Marcos loyalists and more skeptical about the recognition of the Communist Party. He was unwilling to come out for the removal of the Americans from the bases without holding a national plebiscite on the question.

As always, Doy was looking ahead. The vice-presidency was only a stepping-stone to the presidency, which he felt to be nearly within his grasp. With a respectable nationwide organization (the UNIDO), staffed by seasoned politicians from the former Nacionalista and Liberal camps, he would maneuver to expand his role in the government and to strengthen a Laurel machine to work for him in the next presidential election. He was confident that he could not only draw supporters from the Marcos loyalists but could win the blessing of Washington.

From the moment of the dictator's departure, Minister of Defense Juan Ponce Enrile, who held that position under Marcos and retained it under Aquino, presented an enigma. Never was an erring politician more quickly restored to grace. He had confessed his sins as a pro-Marcos operator. As a civilian lawyer, he had accumulated a substantial fortune in logging, real estate, communications, and the coconut industry. On the other hand, as a military person, he had clashed frequently with General Ver and General Ramos. He pictured himself as the father of the Reform of the Armed Forces Movement, and on American television he referred to selected army officers as "my boys." Disclaiming any intention of creating a military coup, he insisted that he backed Cory to the hilt but made no bones about his disagreements with her: He objected to her sequestration of ill-gotten wealth and disapproved of what he called her appeasement of the NPA. Always forthright in his ambition to be president, his power base in Ilocos Norte provided him with his own private army. He had influential friends in the church hierarchy, and had managed to straddle the issues dividing Marcos and the revolutionary forces.

Other political currents were stirring among the ex-political moderates. Rene Cayetano, a friend of Enrile, was endeavoring to revive the old Nacionalista Party. Old-time leaders of the Liberals, including Jovito "Jovy" Salonga, Eva Estrada Kalaw, and Ninoy's own mother, Dona Aurora Aquino, were attempting to revitalize their party. Such cause-oriented groups as the Coalition for the Restoration of Democracy, the Concerned Women of the Philippines, the League of Filipino Students, and the Alliance of Concerned Teachers were actively looking for new associations or affiliations.

Meanwhile, the extreme left reminded the nation at large that its adherents were not only fighting in the hills, but that they also had a program for political action. The National Democratic Front (NDF), the Communist Party of the Philippines (CPP), and the New People's Army (NPA) jointly addressed their special appeals to the radical elements among the youth, the students and teachers, the labor unions, the tribal minorities, and the priests and nuns who leaned toward liberation theology. Their appeals would become stronger unless the Filipinos under Cory were to succeed in getting their political act together.

THE ECONOMIC
DIMENSION

The economic crisis that Marcos left as his legacy constituted the major obstacle to the rehabilitation goals of the Aquino administration: a government completely discredited and deeply in debt, with production curtailed and trade stagnated, and 70 percent of the country's people existing at the poverty line without hope for a better future. To hold Marcos responsible for much of the distress in the Philippines was certainly justified, for during his term in office he had assumed total power and total responsibility for national development as well as for political governance.

When Marcos came to power in 1965, the Philippines was considerably ahead of Thailand, Indonesia, and even South Korea, in terms of income per person, growth rate of GNP, and control of inflation. When he departed, the Philippines lagged behind all three. In 1965 the Philippines was the equal of South Korea in exports; in 1985, South Korean exports were seven times those of the Philippines. Under Marcos, the Philippines sank from second to Japan (in Asia) in economic progress to second-to-none in poverty and despair. "The only turtle in the Asian sea of flying fish," it was the only ASEAN country with a negative growth rate of its GNP. In the meantime, the Philippine population continued to grow at an alarming rate, doubling during the 20 years that Marcos was in power from 27 million to some 55 million.

From the beginning, Marcos equated political power with economic power. The vast machinery of his office operated under that reality. Policies were drawn, laws enacted, organizations created, relationships rearranged, rights and obligations defined, always with the thought in mind that he who controls the coffers controls the crown. All the graft and corruption of the old regime continued in the "New Society," but they became more pervasive, more efficient, and more centrally controlled. With the proclamation of martial law, Marcos had sought to dismantle the economy and reconstitute it under his own relatives and his trusted friends—or under political kingpins in regions where he wanted to get rid of his political opposition. He arrested some oligarchs and simply seized the property of others. He destroyed the Osmenas, the Lopezes, and the Jacintos; he favored the Elizaldes. He created a new elite of multimillionaires. Casting aside the traditional conservatism of the Philippine government, he appointed a select group of technocrats to implement the economic aspects of his "revolution" from above. Private enterprise was pushed aside to make way for state capitalism. The concentration of power in the hands of the government and the exercise of governmental functions to favor his friends were the basic causes of economic disaster.

THE AGRICULTURAL
DISASTER

The principal charge of economic incompetence against Marcos was his mismanagement of Philippine agriculture. Agriculture, including livestock, forestry, and fish, provided all or part of the income of three-fourths of the nation's workforce and almost half of its export earnings, yet it accounted for only one-fourth of its gross domestic product. Rice and corn were the main subsistence crops; coconuts, sugar, tobacco, bananas, and pineapples were its primary sources of foreign exchange. With about 50,000 square miles of hardwood forests and half again as much area in mineral lands; with rich reserves of gold, silver, copper, nickel, lead, manganese, and zinc, and the world's largest deposits of chromite, the Philippines had no excuse for rural poverty.

Under Marcos, agriculture generally suffered from such discriminatory economic policies as an overvalued currency, heavy export taxes, and pervasive price controls. State monopolies in grains, meat, fertilizer, and particularly in coconut and sugar, were created to strengthen Marcos politically rather than to benefit the farmers. The concentration of power in the hands of the central government prevented the operation of market forces. The flood of Marcos decrees and letters of instruction, plus the exactions of the local officials, made it practically impossible to run a farm or plantation for profit. The cruelties of the undisciplined military and the barbarities of the NPA increased with the deepening poverty of the countryside.

The much heralded Marcos program of land reform in the rice and corn lands was discredited by mismanagement and lack of integrity on the part of the bureaucracy. Instead of millions, only 132,000 tenants in thirteen years were offered title to the land they tilled. They were told that the land would become theirs on payment of fifteen annual installments, yet more than 90 percent inevitably fell hopelessly behind in meeting their schedules. The tenants discovered very quickly that without capital, land distribution did not automatically increase productivity. Marcos's paper decrees could not overcome landlord resistance and tenant helplessness to provide a decent living for the rapidly growing rural population.

Although the rice-growing areas had been most favored by the Marcos program of strengthening the infrastructure of roads, wells, bridges, highways, and electrification, rice production was not much greater in 1985 than it had been in 1980. In that time the population of the Philippines had increased by 5 million people. The Philippines had become self-sufficient in rice but only by maintaining an extremely low level of consumption. Very little of the billions of dollars earned annually by agricultural exporters trickled down to individual planters and farmers. Although one-third of the Philippine population derived its living from coconuts, 70 percent of the growers farmed on less than a dozen acres. Most small growers were dirt poor. In the poverty-stricken coconut areas of Mindanao, Samar, and Leyte, the strength of the NPA was, not surprisingly, greatest.

The record of the coconut industry showed Marcos economics at its worst. In 1974, when a shortage of coconut oil drove the prices skyward, Marcos ordered a levy on the coconut producers to subsidize the consumers. He created the Philippine Coconut Authority (PCA) under the chairmanship of his close friend and confidante, Minister of Defense Enrile. The mission of the PCA was to strengthen the Philippine position in world markets and to revitalize the domestic industry by replacing old coconut trees with a new, high-yielding variety. One of the directors of the PCA was Danding Cojuangco, a fraternity brother of Marcos, the baptismal godfather of Marcos's only son, a cousin of Cory Aquino, and himself a sugar and banking tycoon from Tarlac. Cojuangco was given the contract to supply the seedlings for the new type trees (a hybrid, "Mawa," of Malayan and West African varieties), netting him an annual profit running into millions of dollars.

The magnitude of the coconut financial operations necessitated an in-house bank, whereupon the Cojuangco family's First United Bank in 1975 became the United Coconut Planters Bank (UCPB). Cojuangco became a 10 percent shareholder and profit-sharing president of the bank. Enrile was named chairman of the board. All the funds of the coconut levy and the coconut replanting funds were deposited, interest free, in the bank, which in turn used those deposits for loans (with interest, of course) to coconut farmers.

In April 1977, five of Enrile's former law partners incorporated a private firm, United Coconut Mills (UNICOM), in which the UCPB became a heavy investor. Cojuangco was made president of UNI-COM, to which Marcos had given the responsibility for the buying, milling, and marketing of copra. Enrile, Cojuangco, the PCA, the UCPB, and UNICOM all made money—lots of it—while the planters were ripped off and the workers suffered. A group of economists from the University of the Philippines estimated that the growers received no more than half the money to which they were entitled. Cojuangco, Enrile, and their accomplices, undoubtedly including Marcos, ran the monopoly of the biggest industry in the country with the dual purpose of maximizing their own profits and destroying their political rivals in coconut country.

After 1983, when the bottom dropped out of the export market for copra and coconut oil, the misdeeds of the coconut monopoly were brought to light. The magnitude of its manipulations could only be guessed, since its accounting methods were highly imaginative and its books were not subject to public audit.

The case of sugar was as blatant as that of coconut. In contrast to coconut, which is grown on small farms, sugar may be grown on small or large plantations. Of some 33,000 plantations (primarily in Negros, Panay, and Tarlac), a mere 600 plantations controlled half of the entire sugar output. Sixty percent of the farms were less than 12.5 acres; 20,000 farms together had only 12 percent of the sugar lands. Cory Aquino's Hacienda Luisita was one of the larger plantations, employing some 6,000 workers. For years, growing sugar was an easy way of life for the plantation owners. The financial risks were assumed and the markets assured by the government. The workers demanded, and expected, nothing more from the growers than food, shelter, and a reasonable livelihood for their children. As long as sugar prospered, the Philippines seemed immune to the revolution of rising expectations.

In a diet-conscious world, sugar became a sunset industry. Philippine sugar prospered until it lost the American market with the expiration of its quota in 1974. At that time Marcos made Bobby Benedicto, a classmate and fraternity brother of his at the University of the Philippines Law School, the sugar czar. (He was ambassador to Japan when called to head the sugar monopoly.) As head of the Philippine Sugar Commission (PHILSUCOM) and the National Sugar Trading Company (NASUTRA), and major stockholder in the Republic Planters Bank, he was given the authority to negotiate and handle all contracts for the purchase, milling, and sale of sugar. During a decade of operations, Benedicto was accused of market and financial manipulation for personal benefit, resulting (according to the University of the Philippines economists) in losses of between P 11 billion* (the value of the peso ranged from seven pesos to one dollar in 1981 to twenty pesos to one dollar in 1985) and P 14 billion to the sugar producers. That the planters increasingly rebelled against the government and that the workers turned against both the planters and the government was hardly surprising.

At Marcos's departure, the sugar lands presented an unrelieved panorama of hunger and distress. While sugar brought no more than five cents per pound on the world market, the cost of production in Negros was nearly three times that much. As exports dwindled, mills closed. The sugar barons lost their luxurious way of life. The workers lost their jobs. Half of the entire sugar workforce was on part time, and one worker out of five had no work at all. With no land and no credit, their families were forced to live on a starvation diet of grass soup, root crops, and bananas. The evidence of poverty was on every street corner in Bacolod. Many would have starved had it not been for the church, UNICEF, and thousands of individuals from all over the world who showed in a substantial way that they cared.

THE INDUSTRIAL FAILURE

The Marcos failures in agriculture were matched by his mishandling of the nation's industrial development. As Cory expressed it, "The unholy union of insatiable greed and limitless power, of mindless borrowing and reckless expenditure, explains the virtual collapse of the Philippine economy: he [Marcos] has taken us to the waiting room of the world bank with an empty basket in our lap." She accused him of piling up fortunes for his family and friends rather than assuring the welfare of the Philippine people.

Before martial law the Filipino people, with their entrepreneurial talent and pool of skilled labor, made satisfactory progress in expanding the manufacturing segment of the national economy. They followed the rules of an open, competitive market system and adhered to the principles of political democracy. They made the most of their scarce resources. They were able to provide a rising level of living for their growing population and to press forward in the struggle for a

---

*P = pesos.

higher standard of social justice without endangering their lives or jeopardizing their civil liberties.

Matters were entirely different under the martial law regime of Marcos. His fumbling, corrupt government stifled entrepreneurship, and his bureaucratic red tape turned ordinary business life into a nightmare. He lavished favors and privileges on individuals and corporations without holding them accountable for their conduct or obliging them to meet the market tests for efficiency and survivability. The consequent alienation of the middle class was a major cause of his ultimate downfall.

In the aftermath of the Vietnam War, the counsel for self-reliance contained in the Nixon doctrine, and the oil crisis of 1973, Marcos had shared the determination of other national leaders in Asia to modernize their economies as quickly as possible. Convinced that rapid progress could not be attained under the conservative oligarchs and traditional import-substitution policies, he concentrated all decision-making power for national development in his own hands and launched an expansive program designed to stimulate demand and production. He would go head-over-heels in debt if necessary to build highways, dams, bridges, public buildings, shopping centers, hotels, and monuments—the outward symbols of progress. The mania to expand hypnotized him, and the world was filled with dollars to be borrowed—with hefty commissions and interest charges, to be sure. Mrs. Marcos once remarked to me, "Funny people, you Americans— you stuff money down our throats and you expect us to pay it back."

Through the 1970s the GNP of the Philippines grew at an annual rate of 6 percent. With funds obtained from abroad, the state banks— staffed by Marcos—made heavy equity investments in selected private enterprises. For example, in 1973–74, Marcos granted an exclusive timber concession on 500,000 acres of communally owned Tingguian tribal lands in Northern Luzon, plus rights to build and operate a pulp mill, to Cellophil Resources Corporation and to a sister company headed by his friend and golfing partner, Herminio Disini. Because the tribesmen opposed the project, Marcos sent units from the constabulary and the Presidential Security Command to protect the company. The NPA backed the Tingguian tribesmen. In four hectic years the mill was completed, but in 1980 communist terror forced it to close down. Trucks were pushed down ravines, bulldozers were burned, camps raided, and soldiers ambushed and killed. Since Marcos had underwritten the firm's foreign financing, the Development

Bank of the Philippines found itself at the time of his departure with a $200 million equity in a worthless, nonfunctioning papermill.

Using this same Herminio Disini, Marcos negotiated with Westinghouse for the construction of a 620-megawatt nuclear power plant to be built by its Swiss subsidiary at Bataan, some 60 miles northwest of Manila. Its cost was estimated at $1.1 billion, of which half was to be supplied by the U.S. Import-Export Bank and the remainder by Citicorp, Swiss, and Japanese Banks. When completed, it cost twice that amount. With Marcos gone, the plant was mothballed, at a cost to the government of $335,000 per day in interest charges alone.

Another example of an economic fantasy that failed to materialize was that of Rodolfo Cuenca, whose conglomerate, the Construction and Development Corporation of the Philippines (CDCP), at one time had over $1 billion in contracts for roads, dams, bridges, viaducts, drainage systems, power and communications installations, and traffic control systems—not only in the Philippines but all over Southeast Asia and as far afield as Africa and Saudi Arabia. The CDCP built the Manila Light Transit System, the coastal highway from Manila to Cavite, and drained the Manila baylands. It owned a shipping line, mining properties, insurance companies, and real estate in San Francisco (all with Marcos's blessing). When it went bankrupt in 1983, it defaulted on $700 million in government credits and bank loans. More than 20 percent of the nation's money supply was needed to take over CDCP's debt.

The full extent of the damage done to the country by Marcos economics was only partially uncovered at the time of his departure. What was known from court records and the direct testimony of former associates was only the tip of the iceberg. Billions of dollars in currency, securities, and real estate were involved in the obscure operations of personal confidantes, offshore holding companies, and dummy corporations. Marcos himself was linked to the Herald Center and three condominiums on Fifth Avenue in Manhattan, the Lindemere estate on Long Island, and a thirteen-acre home on the Princeton Pike. He had taken excellent care of his younger brother, his sister, and his uncle, and provided lavishly for his children—"Bong Bong," Imee, and Irene. His bank accounts were shrouded in mystery.

Imelda's extravagant tastes and escapades need no further elucidation. Her own family—the Romualdez family of Leyte—was no less grasping than the Marcos family. Her brother, Kokoy, the governor of Leyte and former ambassador to Washington (who was never there), acquired wealth in Benguet Mining, the Manila Electric Company, the Philippine Trust Company, the Philippine-American Life Insurance Company, a Manila newspaper, and various transport companies. Brother Bojo was set up in the Bataan Shipyards and the gambling casinos. Sister Alita and her husband, Rodolfo "Rudy" Martel, were made partners in shopping centers, plush hotels, the steel combine, and the jai alai fronton in Manila.

While the Marcoses ran the economy, their friends and cronies prospered. Danding Cojuangco, in addition to his coconut bonanza, became chairman of the board of the San Miguel Brewing Company. With his interests in real estate, horses, fighting cocks, jewelry, shipping, cement, banking, and international trade, Cojuangco became, after Marcos, the second most powerful man in the Philippines. It was said that he did not wish to run the country, he only wanted to own it. Bobby Benedicto's fortunes grew as long as Marcos remained in office. From sugar, he expanded into banking and shipping; he bought controlling interest in a radio and television network, a luxury hotel, and a major Manila newspaper, the *Daily Express*.

Other members of the inner circle whose wealth depended on presidential favoritism included Ramon (Jun) Cruz, the manager of the Government Social Insurance Service and president of Philippine Air Lines (PAL). Without concern for profit or loss, he ran PAL as though it were his own fleet of flying yachts. (He had to accommodate Imelda whenever she demanded a Boeing 747 or a DC-10 for one of her special safaris.)

Then there was Ricardo Silverio, engaged with his Japanese friends in as many as thirty companies in textiles and motors; Jose Y. Campos, an ethnic Chinese financial adviser to Marcos, known as the drug king, who reputedly owned properties running into the millions in Seattle and Vancouver; Antonio Floirendo, who made his millions in sugar refining in Brooklyn and in a banana trade made lucrative by access to cheap labor and the cheap land rentals of the Davao Penal Colony; Geronimo Velasco, former head of Dole Philippines and minister of energy resources, who supplied meat for the armed forces of the Philippines and for the luxury hotels in Manila from his ranch in Palawan—and who supposedly took a substantial slice out of the purchase price paid for every barrel of oil coming into the Philippines; Luis Villafuerte, minister of trade, whose rackets included the recruitment and training (bribery) of overseas workers, especially those going to the Middle East; and finally, Romeo Espino, the longest overstaying general in the history of the armed forces of the Philippines, whose extracurricular activities extended into insurance, marketing, broadcasting, hotels, steel, chemicals, and mining.

The activities of the Marcos cronies penetrated to the very roots of the Philippine economy. They engaged in kickbacks and payoffs. They evaded taxes and salted their dollars abroad. They funded elections and maintained their own private armies. Through mismanagement, waste, and skimming off profits for themselves, their enterprises fell into such disarray that the government had to bail them out. It was generally believed that Marcos and his favorites had captured for their own benefit more than half the assets of the entire country.

Marcos carried on with his overly ambitious development plans long after he should have realized that they were doomed from the start. Early in the 1980s he projected new plants for steel, cement, phosphate fertilizer, petrochemicals, cocochemicals, diesel engines, heavy machinery, copper-smelting, and aluminum-smelting. He established a free trade zone on the Bataan peninsula to encourage exports and sought further to reduce his country's dependence on foreign oil by adding an alcogas plant and geothermal and hydroelectric powerhouses to the nuclear power plant he had under construction. Together, including 10 to 30 percent for hidden corruption taxes, these projects were expected to cost in the neighborhood of $4 billion.

FINANCIAL COLLAPSE

Most of the projects undertaken were economically unjustifiable, requiring more capital, more high technology, and more entrepreneurial and management skills than the Philippines could supply. Most were never completed, some were dropped after inauspicious beginnings, and none entered into profitable production. The government's loss of political credibility was compounded by its lack of sound economic judgment. As the sources of credit tightened, interest rates soared. The government budget and the international income account sank deeper into the red. One after another the public companies failed. Construction stopped and trade dried up. Even before the assassination of Ninoy Aquino in 1983, Marcos had brought the Philippines to an economic dead-end.

The sums he borrowed were not massive in the context of world totals, but they were insupportable in terms of the limited Philippine resources. When, after inaugurating martial law, Marcos started his borrowing spree, the foreign debt of the country was a mere $2.2 billion. It reached $14 billion by the end of 1981, and $24.6 billion when, in October 1983, the Philippines announced its first moratorium. Of that total, 60 percent was owed to private commercial banks, 16 percent to such multilateral agencies as the ADB (Asia Development Bank), the IMF (International Money Fund), and the World Bank, and the remainder to short-term suppliers of credit for export-import trade. It was a popular guess that $6 or $7 billion of the $24.6 billion total had been dissipated, or absorbed, by the malfeasance of Marcos and his favored friends. In the period immediately following Ninoy's assassination (August 21, 1983) and the debt moratorium (October 17, 1983), the combined political and economic crises sounded the first clear notes of the impending fate of the Marcos regime.

Not a shred of confidence was retained in the ailing ruler. Foreign firms made no further investments in the country and Filipinos sent their capital abroad as fast as they could. Government banks and nonfinancial institutions were forced to take over the bad debts of such public corporations as the National Power Company, the Philippine National Oil Company, the National Electrification Administration, the Metro Manila Transit Corporation, the Light Rail Transit Authority, the National Irrigation Administration, the Metropolitan Waterworks, and the National Housing Authority. The list was endless.

The GNP of the Philippines declined by 6 percent in 1984 and another 5 percent in 1985. As budget deficits mounted and exports could not hope to meet the annual interest bills of $2.5 to $2.8 billion, Marcos turned to his foreign creditors for further relief. But the foreign commercial banks, the official lending agencies, and the multilateral institutions were all turned off by his dismal record. Lacking any confidence whatever in his integrity, they were not disposed to make any funds available to him without the strictest possible controls. Their attitude toward the Philippines was expected to be negative for as long as Marcos remained in office.

Protracted negotiations were carried on by the Philippines with all its creditors. In December 1984 and May 1985, agreements were reached that provided money for the Philippines to pay its overdue debts and made new credits available for reopening the clogged channels of trade. In order to avail himself of the new credits, Marcos was obliged to accept a set of stringent conditions imposed by the key lender, the IMF. Onerous exchange regulations would have to be lifted and the peso allowed to float. The Philippines would have to reform its tariff and tax laws, abandon a wide range of price controls, abolish the agricultural monopolies, and curb the deficits in the budget and the international income account. It was obligated to keep a tight rein on the money supply and to keep inflation under control.

This was bitter medicine for Marcos to swallow. He had lived by the code of spending and reckless expansion and now, at the end of his rule, he was forced to accept a strict regime of belt-tightening and fiscal austerity. With the conditions of grace obtained from his commercial creditors, and with almost $2 billion that he was able to wangle in government-to-government assistance, Marcos felt he was secure until the end of 1986. But the gods willed it otherwise.

The official figures of loans and deficits were only part of the economic story when Marcos left office. With total power and total responsibility, he had brought domestic business to a practical standstill and plunged his people deep into despair. The Development Bank of the Philippines found itself with $25 billion in assets tied up in 122 bankrupt companies and with payments not made on $17 billion (65 percent) of its loans. The Philippine National Bank was equally hamstrung. The National Development Company held an equity interest in over fifty distressed firms, while the National Investment Company and the Government Social Insurance carried over $3 billion in questionable investment on the books. In international trade and finance, the Philippines had been discredited to the point where it could only regain its good standing by hard work and the enlightened cooperation of its creditors.

The wretchedness of the Marcos economic heritage was evidenced even more by the prevalence of human misery than by gloomy statistics. The signs of suffering were deeply etched in the faces of the poverty-stricken people in Manila, in the provincial towns, and in the countryside. Seventy percent of all Filipinos lived under the subsistence level of $100 per month. Even if all the average household's income were allotted for food alone—without counting expenses for clothing, water, education, and transportation—each person had less than 55 cents to spend per day.

In Manila, the homeless slept in the streets or in the shadows of the tourist hotels. Squatters' slums, like Tondo or Binondo, sheltered far more people than the mansions of Forbes Park, Dasmarinas, or suburban Alabang. The glamorous facade of Makati was no substitute for the neglect into which downtown Manila had fallen. In sections that were once prosperous, small boys and old ladies peddled lottery tickets, cigarettes, newspapers, or sampaguita flowers for a pittance. Or they begged persistently for a peso "because I am hungry." Unfortunately, Manila was the prototype for the entire country.

The full burden of hard times rested heavily on the shoulders of the poor, the homeless, and the hungry. As prices of rice, fish, salt, cooking oil, chicken, and pork spiraled upward, the heartbreak and the suffering of the poor increased. And the country edged closer to a real social revolution. With unemployment at 15 percent and underemployment three times that high, the urban labor force joined with the students and their impoverished country cousins in listening to voices of social protest. The NPA soon found areas of operations in the cities and towns as responsive as those it had previously found in the countryside.

When Marcos departed from the Philippines, the linkage between the politics and the economics of his legacy was crystal clear. In politics, he left confusion and instability; in economics, he left bankruptcy, poverty, and social injustice. The inescapable fact was that the new administration could do absolutely nothing for the future of the Philippines without the restoration of a decent government and an immediate all-out attack on prevailing poverty.

4

"I thought we could reconcile
everybody but some do not want to be
reconciled. I will not give
freedom to those who want to make
trouble for us."

President Aquino

A FRESH START

No one realized better than the new president the magnitude of the problems she had inherited. "I do not promise you miracles," she said. "I will exert all my efforts to eliminate the social cancer of graft and corruption and to establish an honest, efficient, and just system of public service. What belongs to the people will be given back to the people, and those who belong in Muntinglupa [the state prison] will be given suitable quarters in Muntinglupa; I offer you an invitation to hard work and a united struggle. A people deserves the government it gets, but I believe we deserve a better government than we have got."

It was a new experience for Filipinos to find a leader who was an untarnished symbol of integrity. Many were ecstatic; others were skeptical, unable to believe that the old patterns would be obliterated. "Right now we don't know who to pay our dues to, or who we have to bribe. We don't know whose door to knock on to get what we need." The fighting lady in the yellow dress with the astounding poll appeal quickly showed that she intended to take command and that she was perfectly capable of doing so. She set to work to legitimize her own regime, to organize an effective administrative apparatus, to dismantle the Marcos machinery, and to launch her own program of political, military, and economic reform.

POLITICAL
INITIATIVES

In her first proclamation, within days after her inauguration, she announced, "On the basis of the people's mandate clearly manifested last February 7, I and Salvador H. Laurel are taking power in the name and by the will of the Filipino people." As president she was pledged to give priority to measures that would completely reorganize the government, make effective the guarantee of human rights, rehabilitate the economy, promote the national aspirations of the people, recover the properties dishonestly amassed by the leaders and supporters of the previous regime, sequester or freeze their assets, eradicate graft and corruption, restore peace and order, settle the problem of insurgency, and pursue national reconciliation based on justice.

On March 25 the new president replaced the old Marcos constitution with an interim freedom constitution, to remain in effect until a new and regular constitution could be drawn up and accepted by the people. She dissolved the Marcos dominated National Assembly and reserved for herself, but only temporarily, the privilege Marcos had reserved for himself of making laws and treaties, and appointing whom she pleased to government positions. She also reserved for herself the right to appoint local officials—to be known as officers in charge (OICs)—who would hold office until new local officials could be legally elected. She set up a procedure for presidential succession: In the event that she should die, resign, or suffer incapacity, Vice-President Laurel would succeed her. In the event of his incapacity, the cabinet would select one of its own to carry on.

Pleading that time was too precious to permit election for delegates to a constitutional convention, she appointed a Constitutional Commission (Concom) of fifty distinguished citizens to draft a constitution that could be submitted to a nationwide plebiscite. Concom was expected to avoid controversial questions of policy (such as the disposition of military bases and the treatment of foreign debts) and limit itself to defining the type of democratic government it wished to establish. It would restore the judiciary and the legislature to their respected roles in a system of checks and balances, adopt a parliamentary or congressional government—with one or two chambers as preferred—reaffirm the bill of rights, fix the term of office and limit the powers of the president, and decide whether Aquino and Laurel would be allowed to serve out the full term of six years or be subjected to another election about whose legitimacy there could be no possible question. In view of her previous statement that under no circumstances would she ever run again for any office, the provision for another election was a Machiavellian way for Cory's opponents to remove her quickly from the political scene.

Seeking to make the judiciary independent, President Aquino called for the resignation of Marcos appointees from the Supreme Court, the Intermediate Appellate Courts, and the local Courts of First Instance. Her opponents called this the massacre of the judiciary. All members of the special court that had tried and acquitted General Ver and his fellow conspirators for the murder of Ninoy Aquino and Rolando Galman (his alleged communist assassin) resigned, paving the way for the reopening of the investigation of the Aquino assassination. Cory named former Justice Claudio Teehankee as the new chief justice of the Supreme Court and looked to him for leadership in reconstructing the judiciary.

To convert a small group of relatives, trusted friends, old-line politicians, Marcos-haters, and the new exponents of People Power into an administrative corps responsible for the affairs of government and the general welfare of the people was not easy. Whether or not she appointed them to specific jobs, she had to keep around her the people in whom she had implicit confidence. This included her family; some businessmen on whom she had depended; the "Harvard-Jesuit mafia" of devoutly religious counselors, among them Jaime Ongpin, Father Bernas (the president of Ateneo University), Jose Concepcion (the guiding spirit of NAMFREL), Lourdes Quisumbing (a Catholic educator); Neptali Gonzalez (an up-and-coming young political leader); and a few trusted personal and political advisers, including Joker Arroyo, Jose Diokno, Jovito Salonga, Teodoro Locsin, Jr., and Rene Saguisag.

In naming her cabinet, Cory was obliged to come to terms with political reality. Her task was to select her cabinet from among the available mortals, not from a company of angels. She appointed Joker Arroyo as executive secretary, Teodoro Locsin, Jr. as minister of information, and Rene Saguisag as presidential spokesman. To Vice-President Salvador Laurel she assigned the Ministry of Foreign Affairs, and from among his UNIDO associates she named Neptali

Gonzalez as minister of justice, Ernesto Maceda as minister of natural resources, Bert Romulo as budget minister, and Luis Villafuerte as chairman of the Presidential Commission on Government Reorganization (PCGR). Among her own PDP-Laban partisans she allotted the Ministry of Local Government to Aquilino Pimentel, agriculture to Ramon Mitra, public works to Rogaciano Mercado, and tourism to Jose Gonzalez. The chairmanship of the Presidential Commission on Human Rights went to Jose Diokno, and the chairmanship of the Presidential Commission on Good Government (PCGG) to Jovito Salonga, both honored for their fearless opposition to Marcos.

Although they were not of her party, she kept Marcos's old stalwart, Juan Ponce Enrile, as minister of defense and made General Fidel Ramos chief of staff of the New Armed Forces of the Philippines (NAFP). Jaime Ongpin as minister of finance, Jose Concepcion as minister of trade and industry, and Jose Fernandez as president of the Central Bank constituted her economic brain trust. Other significant appointments included Lourdes Quisumbing, a Catholic educator, as minister of education; Heherton Alvarez, who led the Aquino movement in the United States, as minister of land reform; Augusto Sanchez, a radical labor leader, as minister of labor; and Solita Monsod, an academic economist, as minister of the Economic Planning Board and director general of the National Economic Development Authority (NEDA).

Without adequate time for careful consideration, she had to appoint literally hundreds of persons to vital jobs. To fire all the bureaucrats and civil servants tarred with the Marcos brush was impossible; he had made all appointments for the past twenty years. She allowed incumbent officeholders to stay on their jobs until they were replaced by a specific executive order; she had no choice, however, but to get rid of those who could not be expected to go along with her policies. When she set about to appoint new officers in charge (OICs) at the provincial, town, and barangay levels, she ran into unexpected troubles. These are traditionally the arenas where favorite sons struggle for territorial rights, with each contestant having some sort of local support from his family, his tenants or workers, his church, or his hired guns. Family feuds are endemic to Philippine politics.

The incumbents in local offices under Marcos had built up their own power bases, many with private armies. They were not about to step aside without a fight or at least an argument. Having been elected "legitimately" in 1980 and having enjoyed the largesse and

support of Malacañang during their tenure, they believed their bail-
iwicks to be impregnable. Some tried to come to terms with the new
regime, others refused to surrender their offices. In Vigan, Ilocos
Sur (Marcos's home country), the former governor declared, "We will
never allow an officer in charge to invade our province." In Cebu
province, a local warlord stayed ominously away from the turnover
ceremony; in Lanao del Sur, in Muslim territory, the former governor
received his successor with smiles but let him know there would be
the devil to pay if he tried to take over the arms in his private arsenal.
Many if not most of the new OICs assumed office in an explosive
environment.

THE BEGINNINGS
OF REFORM

While the battle over appointments was raging, Cory, as president, demonstrated a capacity for effective action in spite of
inevitable criticism. Within a week of assuming office, she had restored the writ of habeas corpus and had empowered the Presidential
Commission on Human Rights to "investigate complaints, unex-
plained or forced disappearances, extra-judicial killings [salvaging],
massacres, torture, hamleting [forcing people to live in militarily
controlled hamlets], and food blockades." In accordance with her
campaign promises, she released more than 500 political prisoners,
including Jose Maria Sison (chairman of the Communist Party of the
Philippines), Bernabe Buscayno (commander of the NPA), and Hora-
cio "Boy" Morales (a leader of the National Democratic Front). She
scrapped the government's control of the press and moved toward
abolishing the Ministry of Information and Imelda's Ministry of Human Settlements. Against the advice of the military, she held out the
possibility for a cease-fire with the NPA and offered amnesty to any
insurgent who would renounce violence.

Concentrating on strengthening her ties with her people, she frequently spoke at rallies asking that they be patient in their demands
on the government. In acts and deeds she showed her concern for the
poor and the underprivileged. Her living-room chats were featured
fortnightly on television. She opened Malacañang for visitors, converting the former palace into a kind of popular museum. She took
cabinet members with her on political safaris to Davao and Cebu,
thus exposing her government to the people in the provinces as well
as to those in Manila. She talked over problems of government with

local officials and listened to grievances presented by a delegation of the NPA. These were steps that Marcos had never taken.

In handling specific interest groups, the new president tried to do the opposite of what she thought Marcos would have done. To the teachers, she made it clear that while she would like to grant their demand for a 10 percent pay hike, there simply was no money in the budget. Her speech to a conference of management and labor, instead of a two-hour, Marcos-type harangue, was vintage Aquino. To management she said: "You said get rid of Marcos and we will get the economy moving, yet you keep your money in the United States and do not invest in the Philippines," and to labor, "You said all you want is the dignity of labor. . . . O.K., you have it; now get to work."

The military received her special attention. She visited the wounded and sick in military hospitals and passed out awards and medals for deeds of valor. In addressing the graduates of the Philippine Military Academy, she extolled the Reform of the Armed Forces Movement but reminded the cadets that she was establishing a special commission to investigate past abuses and recommend further military reforms. Her candor and sympathetic understanding went far toward winning the confidence of the professional soldiers.

In economic affairs her primary concerns—in sharp contrast to those of Marcos—were mass poverty, massive unemployment, and the inequitable distribution of wealth between the rich and the poor. In attacking these problems she could not hope for quick, spectacular results. The evils were too deeply rooted in Philippine society. To begin a new program for land reform, she could do little more than describe her concepts and indicate her good intentions. Through administering her own hacienda, she had become intimately acquainted with the problems of tenancy, landlessness, and lack of an adequate rural economic infrastructure. Well-informed by her own advisers of the special miseries of Negros, Panay, Samar, and Mindanao, she hurriedly put together a team of dedicated officials, public-minded businessmen, landlords, and church leaders and looked to them to initiate measures against rural poverty.

For the immediate task of providing food for hungry people, she sought aid wherever she could find it. To put as many of the unemployed as possible to work, she authorized additional expenditures for public works despite the strictures of the IMF. In a reversal of the Marcos priorities, she set as her policy first to stimulate growth and then to worry about the effects of increased expenditures on the size of the government deficit. She lost no time in dismantling the crippling agricultural monopolies. Meat, fertilizers, and grain, together with coconuts and sugar, were immediately allowed to move on the free market, subject to whatever price the sellers could command.

The formula agreed upon by her economic brain trust for stimulating industry and trade was to get the government out of business and to maximize the role of private enterprise. To utilize the unused 60 percent of industrial capacity, she removed many restrictions on imported raw materials and reduced taxes on Philippine exports. New credits were sought and obtained to unclog the channels of trade.

To reduce the burden of the horrendous foreign debt, she obtained a standby credit facility of $700 million (U.S. currency) from the IMF, which served as a trigger for separate releases from some of the nearly 500 foreign bank creditors. As the economy showed signs of revival, foreign currency reserves picked up, and some of the Philippine capital on deposit abroad found its way back home. As the credit rating of the country achieved substantial improvement, the United States, Japan, West Germany, Australia, and the European Economic Community came forward with generous offers of development assistance.

Foreign investments were courted, but, as Minister Ongpin said, "We will not stand on our heads to attract them." Cory insisted on protecting the rights of labor and guaranteeing Filipinos a reasonable share of the profits derived from joint ventures. In keeping with traditional practice, she reserved the nation's natural resources and public utilities for exclusive Philippine control. Investment interest picked up to a surprising degree, but improvement was as slow in the industrial sector as it was in agriculture. The political climate remained too uncertain and the opportunities for profit too limited to inspire foreign investors to rush in where Filipino entrepreneurs themselves seemed hesitant and overcautious.

Although Cory believes that the private sector should be the engine of progress, she also believes that the government has a role to play in safeguarding the interests of the poor and in acting as the conscience of the marketplace. She ordered the disposal of the government's equity in 129 state firms that had gone bankrupt, and directed the Development Bank of the Philippines and the Philippine National Bank to liquidate their non-performing assets. Bargains became available in city real estate, huge industrial projects, mining ventures, vast holdings of undeveloped rural lands, coconut oil mills, sugar mills, and luxury hotels.

The Aquino administration was understandably baffled by the problem of the nuclear power plant. An anti-graft league in Manila filed criminal and civil charges against Marcos, the former Energy Minister Geronimo Velasco, and a dozen others, including officials of the Westinghouse Corporation, for allegedly receiving more than $500 million (U.S. currency) in kickbacks and overpricing in the construction of the power plant and the acquisition of equipment. Westinghouse argued that the plant was ready to go and should be put into operation, but a panel appointed by President Aquino insisted that it was too dangerous, especially in light of the Chernobyl incident. While the two sides negotiated, the power plant remained idle, consuming its daily millions in interest and maintenance costs.

Salonga's Presidential Commission on Good Government (PCGG) displayed the utmost vigor in attempting to recover the ill-gotten wealth of the deposed dictator and his family, relatives, and subordinates. Their assets were to be frozen or sequestered, with ultimate disposition to depend on due process of the law. In addition, over 100 persons were put on "hold" orders, preventing them from leaving the country while their accounts were under investigation.

In going after Marcos, the fourteen members of his immediate family, and twenty-four other relatives, the PCGG claimed to have identified $900 million out of the $5 to $10 billion (U.S. currency) he was accused of salting away. While his assets in the Philippines were immediately confiscated, the fate of his properties abroad would depend on the judgments of the courts of the various nations involved. Of the thirty tycoons or cronies listed as his principal subordinates, Danding Cojuangco had sixteen companies sequestered, including some 55 million shares of the San Miguel Brewing Company. Bobby Benedicto lost twenty businesses, mostly in his communications empire, and Antonio Floirendo had to turn over eighteen companies in his conglomerate to the PCGG. In the first hundred days of its operations, the PCGG took in P 1.4 billion in cash and P 15 billion in real estate and other assets. (Twenty Philippine pesos equal one U.S. dollar.)

The "witch-hunt for ill-gotten gains" provoked many serious questions: Should the government have the power to go about freezing assets, sequestering property, and putting people on hold just because of a reasonable belief that they had helped in the plundering of the nation's wealth? What had become of the due process of law? Why should Enrile, an obvious crony, escape the clutches of the PCGG? Why should Cojuangco, who had asserted, "I have nothing to hide; I have nothing to be ashamed of.... I was not a front-man for Marcos; I made my money through hard work and honest deals," not have his day in court?

AT
THE CROSSROADS

Politics. At the end of Cory's first year in office, it was clear that the Philippines had registered some progress, however modest, toward stability. The president had solidified her image of trust and integrity. She had maintained the right forces behind her: the morality of the Catholic Church, the common sense of the business community, the patriotism of the good military officers, and the reawakened effervescent spirit of the Filipino people. The country was calmer than it had been, but the government was still one of the shakiest in Asia.

It was not clear, however, whether the country would go forward under the banner of Cory and company or revert to the blemished ways of traditional Philippine democracy. Would the political road ahead lead to stability and progress or to further suffering, chaos, anarchy, a military coup, and possibly a communist takeover?

Cory's method of operation was characterized by some as weak and indecisive, hypocritical and overpretentious. Accused of delegating too much and of dispensing too many favors and appointments to her relatives and friends, she kept a cool head and preserved her patience, in spite of the waves of Philippine passion that surged about her. She may have lacked flamboyance but not vitality or strength of character. When others criticized her methods, she merely said, "This is democracy in action. I have my job to do and I do it."

Many of the presidential appointees did little to cleanse reputations that were still darkened by the shadows of the past. Unable to divorce themselves from the traditional practices of intrigue, petty bickering, artificial posturing, and personal gain, they continued to act as surrogates of the oligarchs, looking after the interests of the leading families to which they belonged. In spite of President Aquino's high standards, she was unable to achieve in so short a time the elimination of graft and corruption from public life.

During that first year of the new regime, every ambitious Filipino politician looking to his political future sought friends or alliances.

The Marcos loyalists laid low, limiting their activities to writing articles against the government or fomenting demonstrations. The conspicuous leaders of the ruling government coalition—PDP-Laban and UNIDO—were most active. Factions within the Laban and PDP weighed the comparative advantage of sticking together or going their separate ways. The problem for the party hacks was how to derive the maximum advantage from Cory's tremendous popularity. Their immediate objective was victory for their respective candidates in the Congressional and local election of 1987; their ultimate goal was to capture the presidency in 1992. Cory's closest advisers, including most of her relatives, tried in vain to persuade her to identify herself exclusively with the Laban party and thus divorce herself from both the PDP and the UNIDO. In their view, if they could convince the public that they alone were the chosen heirs of Cory's mantle, they would undoubtedly gain more votes. Other advisers saw no need to break up a winning team.

Nene Pimentel, as the leader of the PDP, could not afford to dissolve the union with Laban, because his opportunity to press forward with his personal political designs derived wholly from his position in the cabinet. As minister of local government, he appointed OICs who would be under obligation to him should he run for the presidency.

Doy Laurel, feeling slighted and unappreciated by the president, quietly worked to expand the power of his already formidable UNIDO. Not overburdened by his official duties as vice-president or minister of foreign affairs, he found ample opportunity to strengthen the infrastructure of his party by making many discreet appointments. He seemed willing to float on political waters for the next five years if need be, because he was confident that after Cory he was next in line for the presidency.

Well-known leaders of the traditional Nacionalista and Liberal parties bided their time before deciding whether to resusciatate their old organizations or to join up with any of the new groups. Some leftist-oriented individuals launched a new party—Partido ng Bayan, PNB—pretending to be non-communist, although anti-imperial and anti-feudal. The communists strove for unity, by ironing out the differences between those of their leaders who wanted to continue the armed struggle and those who were willing to negotiate peacefully with the government. Minister of Defense Enrile gradually emerged as the rallying point of the Aquino opposition. Although identified with the military, Enrile was not really a military man. A successful lawyer, he had served under Marcos as undersecretary of finance, commissioner of customs, and minister of justice before becoming minister of defense in 1970. His followers included a select group of military officers, former civilian colleagues and associates, practically all the Marcos loyalists, dissatisfied soldiers, businessmen, and dedicated right-winger, nervous over the growth of the communist insurgency.

Enrile made no secret of his conviction that, given the opportunity, he would make a better president than Marcos ever was or Cory ever could be. He built his case against Cory on the argument that her administration was illegitimate. According to him, she threw away her mandate to govern when she terminated the 1973 constitution and arbitrarily abolished the National Assembly. She acted as "a little dictator" in proclaiming a temporary constitution, appointing a committee to draft a new one, "massacring the judiciary," firing "duly elected local officials," and conducting a witch hunt of selected Marcos cronies.

He demanded the removal of liberal cabinet officers who opposed his demands, which included participation of the military in the investigation of alleged atrocities, reinstatement of some of the Marcos holdovers, dismissal of some of the more controversial OICs, a more coherent line against the insurgents, reinstatement of the 1973 constitution, and an early presidential election.

Enjoying his position on center stage, Enrile became, during the year 1986, the stellar attraction at pro-Marcos, anti-communist rallies. He took over the old Marcos line, "It is either me or the communists." In addition to his basic premise that "the only good commie is a dead commie," he tried to give the impression that he was the legitimate spokesman for democracy and for the military, boasting that "If she continues to put the military in a bad light and picture the insurgents as saints, I might lose my patience, and when I lose my patience, I am like Rambo."

Enrile continued to plug his line that communism could be defeated only if Aquino stabilized her government, strengthened the nation's economy, and cleaned up tendencies toward corruption within the government. He pledged to "go on with our fight, even to hell," and went so far as to plot a coup against Cory during her absence in Japan. His resignation as minister of defense was accepted on November 22, leaving him to pursue his ambitions as an ordinary oppositionist politician.

In view of the conflicting interests and diverse backgrounds of those whom Cory originally chose to assist her, it was remarkable that the group was able to stay together as long as it did. Enrile's resignation, not surprisingly, sparked a cabinet shakeup. Two ministers (the minister of public works and highways and the minister of public resources) were replaced, allegedly for incompetence and corruption. Nene Pimentel was eased out not only for his griping at President Cory but also in response to pressure from the military, and Augusto Sanchez was removed as minister of labor for being too radical. The position of Joker Arroyo as chief cabinet secretary was in constant jeopardy because he was believed to be too pro-communist.

At the end of her year in office, it was plain that Cory had continued to make a tremendous impact on the political scene. Her reputation was unsullied, her intentions unchallenged. That Filipinos were playing politics as usual could not be attributed to any failing on her part. She could hardly be expected to change patterns of political action that had been centuries in taking shape. True, she could take a certain measure of pride in her political accomplishments, but she was concerned about her slow progress in overcoming the nation's economic problems.

Economics. Although no significant results had yet emerged from her efforts toward land reform and the alleviation of rural poverty, Cory's administration had lost none of the nation's faith and confidence. The economic future of the Philippines looked slightly more promising at the beginning of 1987 than it had at the beginning of 1986. She was able to halt the nation's downhill economic slide and to post some encouraging signs for the road ahead. The inflation rate flattened out, the swollen interest rates were substantially reduced, and the cost of living actually began to decline. The peso-dollar exchange rate remained fairly constant—nearly 20 to 1. The foreign exchange reserves doubled to about $2.5 billion (U.S. currency), representing about five months' import coverage. The stock market picked up, as did many lines of industrial production. The tax system was overhauled and collections mounted. Import regulations were eased, as more than 100 items were taken off the tariff lists.

To provide jobs for the rural and urban unemployed, the country went on a spending binge. The heavy government deficit was financed by loans and grants from abroad and by an increase in the domestic money supply. Government monetary policy deliberately departed from the austerity prescriptions laid down by the IMF. Both the balance of trade and the current income account improved, thanks largely to foreign loans, debt rescheduling, and the dramatic drop in the price of imported petroleum products. Philippine exports of electronics, clothing, furniture, and wood products increased and the price of copra improved; but the market for sugar and for copper products remained depressed.

In implementing her economic program, Cory followed up on her promise to reduce the role of government in business. She overhauled the charters of the Philippine National Bank and the Development Bank of the Philippines to speed up progress in getting rid of their non-performing assets. Due to excessive red tape, high government transaction fees, and differences of opinion among her advisers, she was unable to finalize as many sales as she had hoped to. Some advisors favored selling the government interest in distressed firms regardless of losses, while others argued it would be better to extend further government aid to some companies if to do so would make them viable.

The government resolved the question by coming up with an attractive plan. It would sell its equity in distressed firms at a substantial discount, provided the buyer would reinvest the acquired assets in the Philippines. Foreign buyers, however, held back, protesting the vagueness of the government regulations and the uncertainties of the political situation. In the background was the lingering fear of reemerging economic nationalism. The president of the American Chamber of Commerce in the Philippines noted that, in the matter of foreign investment, "The dust has not by any means settled, the atmosphere is not yet clear." Although U.S. multinationals alone held between $2.5 and $3.5 billion in the Philippines and would have liked to expand, they were reluctant to bring in new capital. Other foreign private investors, including the Japanese, were as hesitant as the Americans. Any potential investor was bound to hold back until assured that he could operate with safety in a friendly climate and could repatriate his profits.

It is a safe assumption that no one else could have had the impact that President Aquino has had on the national economy in a single year. Whatever upward movement the Philippines achieved was due primarily to foreign assistance, and foreign assistance was forthcoming only because of the new image of her people and her country that she projected. With grace and dignity, she attracted—and on excellent terms—more than $1.2 billion in loans and grants. More than half came from the United States; the rest came from Japan, Singapore, Australia, New Zealand, Denmark, West Germany, and the European Economic Community. No other Philippine leader could have dealt as effectively as she has with presidents and prime ministers, including Reagan, Nakasone, Hawke, Lange, and Lee Kwan Yew.

THE CONSTITUTION
OF 1987

The climax of President Cory's first year in office came on February 2, 1987, with the resounding three-to-one victory for the "yes" side in the plebiscite for the new constitution. The document itself was not at issue. It was impossible for anyone to pass judgment on the 18 articles, 305 sections, and 24,000 words it contained. During the five months the constitution was in print, it was difficult to obtain a copy of the text. There was little time for study or debate. The interest of ordinary people in the constitution was limited to such nebulous questions as "Will it give me more to eat?" or "Will it bring me free education for my children?" They turned to local politicians, priests, or a series of comic books for their answers. Their most persuasive assurances came from Cory herself, who once again took to the hustings and made the plebiscite a popular referendum for her administration.

Her speeches were not legal analyses; nor where they calls to action. They were political declarations. She again demonstrated her crowd magic. At her final rally before perhaps a half-million people in Manila, she had them shouting their approval of her ode to toughness. She said, "You know that I do not want to kill, but also I do not want them to kill us. I am accused of siding with the right, or with the left, but I am only for you, my beloved people. I thought we could reconcile everybody but some do not want to be reconciled. I will not give freedom to those who want to make trouble for us." She also used the old Marcos tactic—wherever she went she announced some new appointment, some new tax break, or a generous grant for a local works project. No wonder that 90 percent of the registered voters turned out to vote and 75 percent voted "yes." It was probably the cleanest, mildest exercise of the franchise in the history of the Philippines.

The Constitution of 1987 is not a revolutionary document. In reverting to the general features of the Commonwealth Constitution of 1935 it identifies the Marcos Constitution of 1973 as an aberration.

The preamble defines its aims: "To secure to ourselves and our posterity the blessings of independence and democracy under the rule of law and a regime of truth, justice, freedom, love, equality and peace." Its Declaration of Principles and State Policies renounces war as an instrument of policy, declares that civilian authority is at all times supreme over the military, and states that "the Philippines, consistent with the national interest, adopts and pursues a policy of freedom from nuclear weapons in its territory." It recognizes the indispensable role of the private sector, encourages private enterprise, and provides incentives to needed investments. It further asserts that the rights of indigenous cultural communities within the framework of national unity and development shall be recognized and promoted by the State.

Once again the Philippines has adopted an American-style democracy with its system of checks and balances. A bicameral legislature, a president as chief executive, and an independent judiciary have been reestablished. Provisions have been adopted that will prevent a future president from becoming another dictator. Under the heading of local government, autonomy has been granted to Muslim Mindanao and to the Cordilleras, the mountain area in northern Luzon.

The new constitution reflects the determination of the Filipinos to develop the national economy so as to derive the maximum benefit for all their people. It provides that the State shall protect Filipino enterprises against unfair competition in promoting agrarian reform and industrialization. In general the State is empowered to do everything possible to make full use of Philippine labor, enhance Philippine productivity, and exercise the strictest control over foreign investments and foreign loans. The 60–40 percent Filipino–foreign equity ratio in the exploration, development, and utilization of natural resources and in the operation of public utilities is still retained.

The greatest concern is shown for social justice and human rights. A Bill of Rights guarantees to Filipinos very much the same rights that we cherish in the United States and thus protects them from the abuses to which the martial law regime subjected them. The social justice clauses mandate the State to afford full protection to labor, encourage and undertake the just distribution of all agricultural lands, protect the rights of fishermen, undertake a continuing program of urban land reform and housing, adopt a comprehensive health program, look after the welfare of working women, and strengthen the institution of the Filipino family.

The sections of the constitution grouped under the headings of General Provisions and Transitory Provisions provide that no member of the military shall engage in any partisan activity except to vote; no member of the armed forces in active service shall be appointed to any civilian position in the government; laws on retirement of military officers shall not allow extension of their service; and the tour of duty of the chief of staff shall not exceed three years except that it may be extended by the president in times of war or other national emergency. It also provides that the State shall establish and maintain one police force, which shall be national in scope and civilian in character, to be administered and controlled by the National Police Commission.

Other provisions fix the dates for congressional and local elections and extend the terms of President Aquino and Vice-President Laurel to June 30, 1992; order the dismantling of private armies and other armed groups not recognized by duly constituted authority; and further order the dissolution or conversion into the regular forces of all paramilitary forces, including the Civilian Home Defense Forces, not consistent with the citizen armed forces established in this constitution. Of particular interest to Americans is the section reading: "After the expiration in 1991 of the Agreement between the Republic of the Philippines and the United States of America concerning Military Bases, foreign military bases, troops, or facilities shall not be allowed in the Philippines except under a treaty duly concurred in by the Senate and, when the Congress so requires, ratified by a majority of votes cast by the people in a national referendum held for that purpose, and recognized as a treaty by the other contracting state."

AN INTERIM ASSESSMENT

The adoption of the constitution marked the "end of the beginning" of the transition from President Marcos to President Aquino. In one short year she had made a significant start toward reversing the course of Philippine history, which for two decades had moved steadily away from democracy and a free enterprise economy. The negative job of dismantling the Marcos totalitarian structure was now complete; and the positive challenge of constructing her own political machine and formulating her own policies would become her sole responsibility. Confirmed in office for another five years, she no longer needed to be tentative in her decisions or initiatives.

The new constitution, although overwhelmingly approved, was far from perfect. It was subject to criticism for not focusing on the major problem of mass poverty, for keeping the traditional elite in power, and for failing to provide permanent relief from foreign economic domination. In the words of a prominent economist, "Our president is captive and hostage to a constitution that while speaking in populist language serves the most elitist ends. It is molded by the very forces which have kept this nation backward, underdeveloped, and perpetually colonized." Whatever its imperfections, the new constitution did, however, give the government a new and solid framework, and a set of rules allowing it to operate in a just and democratic way. Furthermore, if in the future the constitution should prove to be in any respect ambiguous or inadequate it could always be amended or clarified by subsequent legislation or reinterpreted by the courts.

The adoption of the constitution was an appropriate occasion for a preliminary assessment of President Cory's record. While her overwhelming majority in the plebiscite was a clear indication of her popularity, it was not a comparable endorsement of her performance. Her reputation for integrity remained intact. She was still accepted as the symbol of high moral standards in the public service. She was given full credit for bringing to an end the salvage squads, the arbitrary imprisonments, and the shackles of martial law. She reawakened the people's pride in themselves. Having consistently maintained her poise under intense pressure, she faced the future with confidence.

On the negative side, she had failed in certain respects to rise above traditional practices of Philippine politics. She attacked many of her problems with speeches and promises, rather than instigating enforceable programs of action. On her trips to the provinces, she resorted to announcements of new subsidies for local public works to draw louder applause. She never seemed to be in total command of the political forces that swirled about her. As a typical Filipino she was conscious of her debts of obligation and used her appointive power to reward those who had helped her regardless of their talents or abilities.

It was commonly alleged that she had been used by those around her, especially those "steak commandos" (exiles from the Marcos regime who had been living in luxury in the United States) who had rushed home to reclaim their haciendas, estates, companies, and factories from the cronies. Unlike the president, those people had no interest in genuine reform. Dedicated exclusively to their own and their families' welfare and enmeshed in personal vendettas, they fundamentally opposed any rapid change toward a new dispensation. Many predicted that half of Cory's cabinet would desert her to run for Congress and, having regained their seats or their influence in the legislative branch of the government, would make mincemeat of her good intentions. They would use their political know-how and their wealth to reduce the presidency to an institutional eunuch, to the detriment of the national welfare.

There are those—and I am one—who believe that no party or organization, right or left, holds out more hope for a better future than the present administration. With all her shortcomings, President Cory has emerged with far more credibility than her opponents. She is the best, if not the only, hope for a government that will put the welfare of the people first. In politics, as in economics, the road ahead will be bumpy, but with any other leader presently on the horizon it would be far worse. What is more, as long as she is at the helm of the ship of state, her country is assured of a sympathetic hearing abroad.

She has genuinely given her people a fresh start in the restoration of democracy and the revival of the economy, but much more is required. The future is far from clear. It is imperative to follow up on a substantial beginning. Filipinos of unquestioned integrity and proven competency in their chosen fields must come forward to fill the bureaucratic and technocratic positions needed to cope with the nation's multifaceted crisis.

The people of the Philippines cannot help but be concerned about their future. They ask, "Can Cory live up to her high popularity ratings? Can she carry out the reforms she seeks? Does she have the vision, the courage, and the energy to forge ahead? Can she inspire the people to get to work? Can she enlist the support of the rich oligarchs? Can she attract the foreign assistance (not just military assistance) the country needs?"

The newly unleashed free press bombards her with such loaded questions as, "Why does it take forever to reduce the price of fuel? Where is the land reform she talks about? When is the Marcos money coming back? Where is the help she promised for the poor?" The patience of the hungry and the jobless wears thin very quickly. Discontent grows rapidly when the people's basic needs cannot possibly be satisfied. Every job she fills leaves a dozen hopefuls disappointed; everthing she does or fails to do arouses more criticism than support.

And for the revolutionary forces in the Philippines, the appetite grows with the eating.

The constitution is now in force, but she must still face the problems that lie ahead. Her confidence has been bolstered by the results of the plebiscite, but the real work is still before her. She must follow up on her political and economic initiatives, strengthen the forces for law and order, reform the military, put down the Muslim rebellion, and overcome the communist insurgency.

5

"The revolution began
with a bullet—
a bullet fired by a soldier
into the head of my husband."

President Aquino

THE CHALLENGE OF MILITARY REFORM

Nothing looks more peaceful than the calm sea, the sleeping city, and the tranquil landscape that greet the eye when the tropical dawn breaks in the Philippines. But the heat of the day and the cover of the night have contributed to a rate of crime, rebellion, and insurgency that has been the curse of Philippine society and the bane of the Philippine government. If the Filipino people are to make progress in developing their nation, they must be given an environment of peace and security in which to live and work. It is the government's responsibility to provide that environment—a responsibility not easy to fulfill. The problem of law and order will plague President Aquino as it has plagued her predecessors.

Nothing condemns the Philippines more in the eyes of the outside world than its high rate of violent crimes. It may be that the incidence of such crimes is exaggerated by elements in the media that thrive on sensationalism, but the greater likelihood is that far more murders, assaults, and cases of harassment and kidnapping occur than are reported. The grisly slayings of such figures as Mayor Cesar Climaco of Zamboanga, politician Evilio Javier, radical labor leader and president of the leftist Bayang party Rolando Olalia, and chairman of the West Mindanao regional government Ulbert Ulama Tugung are only surface indications of a condition that gnaws at the vitals of Philippine society.

The problems of civil disorder are rooted in both the inequities of Philippine society and the crime-causing factors embedded in its commonly accepted behavior patterns. All too often a Filipino assumes that he can get away with his crime, that he, or a powerful patron, can fix things up because local police and justice authorities are believed to be open to peso persuasion. Some acts that the law defines as crimes—squatting on idle lands, smuggling, and fishing by dynamite—are not regarded as crimes by the mass of ordinary citizens.

Violence is often looked upon as an unavoidable aspect of the political process. That physical assault or murder may result from local factional rivalries and interfamily feuds, and that the right of self-defense justifies the private possession of arms or the utilization of hired hoods or private armies, are accepted facts. To take action on one's own is sometimes considered necessary, because relying on the courts too often means that justice will never be done.

LAW:
MARCOS STYLE

In 1973, after declaring martial law, President Marcos announced that his first concern was to secure the entire citizenry from the criminal elements, the private armies bred by local politics, and the outlaw bands in the countryside. To achieve this end it was imperative, he claimed, to dismantle not only the apparatus of the insurgency movement, but also "the whole system of violence and criminality that had virtually imprisoned our society in fear and anarchy." As safety measures, he ordered all private citizens to turn in their guns and imposed a midnight-to-dawn curfew.

The Marcos method of preserving public order permitted ruthlessness on the part of the police and military authorities, backed by uninhibited use of specialized intelligence and security agencies. Marcos felt no obligation to respect human rights. He suspended the writ of habeas corpus, arrested and detained people with or without cause, and ignored charges of kidnapping, torture, and salvaging (killing) against himself and his military establishment. Personal data acquired through a national registration system were computerized and made available to police and security authorities as a surveillance tool in criminal investigations and in the control of subversive activities. His specialized enforcement agencies were the Presidential Security Command (PSC), the National Intelligence and Security Authority (NISA), the constabulary's Metropolitan Command (Metrocom), the National Bureau of Investigation (NBI), and the Integrated National Police (INP)—all under the command of General Ver, his Chief of Staff.

The PSC was responsible for guarding Marcos and protecting his business interests, such as the Tingguian timber concession. Ver's personal agents were said to be found in every government office, military unit, and major business, and on every college campus. NISA men were sent as attachés to Philippine embassies and consulates in those countries where the largest overseas Filipino communities were located. Ver was personally responsible for the "safe houses" in which detainees were held and interrogated, and where Marcos himself would go when he wanted to get out of everybody's sight.

The more desperate the people became in their demand for a change, the more Marcos increased his repressive measures. To oppose him was to be a criminal. In a system fashioned to keep himself at the top, anyone who threatened him automatically became a subversive. One was either pro-Marcos or a communist; citizens who had a just cause or a legitimate gripe were classed as anti-government. Many Filipinos complained that under Marcos life was worse than it had been under the Japanese.

THE EROSION OF
THE MILITARY TRADITION

Military traditions in the Philippines are based on the American heritage, enriched by such officers as Generals Pershing, Eisenhower, Arthur MacArthur, and his son, Douglas. As long as the United States ruled the Philippines, units of the American forces were maintained in the country to provide for external defense. Among those forces was a separate body called the Philippine Scouts, consisting of Filipino enlisted personnel and U.S. officers.

In 1901, the Philippine Constabulary (PC) was established by the United States to act as an insular police force patterned on military lines. It was at first manned by Filipinos and officered by U.S. personnel, but by the time the Commonwealth was inaugurated in 1935 the PC chief and 96 percent of the officer ranks were Filipinos. The PC's scope of operation was virtually unlimited—from game wardens, jail guards, and postmasters to inspectors of military science courses taught in the schools and colleges and escorts of civilian officials into the back country. The PC was not a military institution *per se*, but its melding of police, paramilitary, and civilian functions provided a model for subsequently created armed forces.

In the Philippines as in the United States, it was traditional that, while on duty, the military were first and foremost professional soldiers—disciplined, committed to God and country, living on their bases, and always subject to the control of civilian authorities. There was no engaging in extraneous political and economic activities in order to amass ill-gotten gains. In World War II, for a Philippine fighter to serve the Americans conferred a badge of honor on him. When independence was regained in 1946, the Philippines set up its own defense establishment, the Armed Forces of the Philippines (AFP), with the advice and assistance of the Americans. The AFP was thoroughly American in tradition, philosophy, training, and equipment.

With the growth of the Huk insurgency in the 1950s, slippage in the quality of the AFP became all too evident. Encouraged and supported by the American embassy, Secretary of Defense Ramon Magsaysay launched a broad program of military reform. By absorbing the Philippine Constabulary (PC), the AFP became the policeman of the nation as well as its defender. By the same token, the PC, as an arm of the military, became eligible for American military assistance and could send its officers to the United States for advanced training. Between 1950 and 1979, more than 16,000 Filipino officers benefited from this integrated arrangement.

The AFP-PC integration pleased the Americans, who wanted stronger allies in containing communism. It also suited Filipinos, except for those extreme nationalists who resented what they saw as further American meddling in Philippine domestic affairs. Secretary Magsaysay got more and better trained fighters against the Huks, and he succeeded in getting the soldiers out of the barracks. He used his men to build roads, bridges, and irrigation ditches in a civic action program designed to attract the Huks to a better life.

Magsaysay also used the soldiers and the constabulary to police the election of 1953. Without his men to guarantee the security of the polling places, monitor the voting process, and watch the counting of the ballots, he would not have been elected to the presidency over his adversary and former boss, President Quirino. In fulfilling its newly assumed role as guardian of democracy, the military recaptured a large part of its tarnished glory.

Between Magsaysay and Marcos, without a domestic crisis to deal with, the military again lost much of its prestige. National defense accounted for only 15 percent of the national budget, with 80 percent of its appropriation going for salaries and retirement. The total force of 50,000 was top-heavy with officers. There were more captains, majors, and lieutenants in service than buck privates, and more sergeants and corporals than pfc's. More Filipinos were on duty in the U.S. Navy than in the Philippine Navy.

The decline of the military in social prestige was matched by the deterioration in the professional standards of the Philippine soldier. He could not devote himself to improving his military skills while he was digging wells. When the brightest of officers discovered that their talents were marketable outside their own profession, they used their military positions and associations as stepping stones to more profitable non-military careers. The military bureaucracy became just as susceptible to graft and corruption as the civil bureaucracy.

THE MILITARY
UNDER MARCOS

As soon as he was elected to the presidency in 1965, Marcos gave the country a preview of the further use he intended to make of the military. Projecting an entire program of national development based on military civic action, he created two engineering battalions, obtaining the necessary equipment from the United States as payment for sending a Philippine Civil Action Group (PHILCAG) to Vietnam. In the eyes of the American government, the showing of the flag of the Philippines, an Asian ally, in the battle zone justified the cost.

Shortly after taking office, President Marcos put in place his security intelligence apparatus, involving the PSC, NISA, and Metrocom, as described above. He increased the size of the armed forces from 45,000 in 1967 to 58,000 in 1971 to maintain order and to counter the Moro rebellion and the NPA. He established the National Defense College, not only to provide advanced military education but also to introduce his senior officers to political, economic, and administrative subjects. Then he used twelve of his most responsible military favorites (the "Twelve Disciples," including Enrile, Ramos, and Ver) to prepare his plans for martial law.

During the period of martial law, he made the structure of the AFP as solid as he could. He tripled the number in service to approximately 60,000 in the regular army, 16,000 in the air force, 98,000 in the navy, and 10,000 in the marines. In addition, he provided for some 43,000 in the Constabulary, 46,000 in the Integrated National Police (INP), 65,000 in the Civil Home Defense Forces (CHDF), and 124,000 in the reserves. The annual budget appropriation grew from $90 million in 1971 to more than $1 billion in 1983, exclusive of the substantial sums received from the United States in military assistance. These figures were not in themselves extravagant inasmuch as the Philippines—with all its problems—was the lowest of all the ASEAN states in percentage of GNP spent on national defense.

What happened to besmirch the record of the AFP and to blight the good name of the military during the Marcos regime was primarily his doing, but those who participated in his schemes, knowingly tolerated his excesses, and profited from his blessing share the blame. Unfortunately, the performance record of the AFP in maintaining law and order was so dismal that local warlords, incipient rebellions, and a mounting, communist-led insurgency threatened—and eventually destroyed—the Marcos mandate to rule. The U.S. government had consistently issued calls for military reforms, but Marcos refused to heed them.

In addition to its basic mission of defending the country against invasion and countering insurgency, the role of the armed forces as Marcos perceived it was to protect him and his family, to enforce the system of martial law, and to assume a dominant role in Philippine life. Minister of Defense Juan Ponce Enrile was the civilian chosen to implement the Marcos philosophy. After a reorganization of the structure of the armed forces to make General Ver chief of staff, Marcos proceeded to convert them into a Praetorian Guard whose first duty was to protect Malacañang as though it were a fortress and to minister to Marcos and his family as though they were sacred. It was the army's misfortune that personal loyalty to Marcos often overrode all sense of duty to God and country.

Ver and Marcos were born in the same hometown, Ver being the younger by two years. Like Marcos, he was a graduate of the University of the Philippines. Completing the ROTC in 1941, he was assigned to the Philippine Constabulary. His record in World War II is a blank. Serving in the ranks of the Constabulary until 1963, he was detailed to Marcos, then president of the Senate. After two years studying police administration in Washington, D.C. and at the University of Louisville in Kentucky, he returned to Manila to become Marcos's chief of security during the presidential campaign of 1965.

The Marcos victory brought about Ver's promotion to major and his appointment as head of the Presidential Guard Battalion. His rise was meteoric. He converted the Presidential Guard into the Presidential Security Command and expanded the National Intelligence and Security Authority into an organization rivaling in scope the Catholic Church or the NPA. As chief of staff, Ver had control over appointments, assignments, salaries, and promotions. The regional commanders and their staffs, especially the PSC and NISA, were stacked with Ver's personal appointees. His three sons occupied sensitive military command positions. A popular story in Manila indicated precisely where Ver's personal loyalties lay: If Marcos were to order Ver to make a suicide leap off a high building, Ver's only question would be, "Which floor, Mr. President?"

Ver's rivals for favor and power were Minister Enrile and the vice-chief of staff and commanding general of the Philippine constabulary, General Fidel Ramos. Enrile was too ambitious to satisfy Marcos. It was convenient to keep Enrile, the sharp lawyer, in the top civilian post, but it would have been dangerous to give him too much authority. Ramos, like Ver and Marcos, was an Ilocano. Unlike Ver, Ramos was a professional soldier. A graduate of West Point, he served with Philippine contingents in Korea and in Vietnam.

Within the armed forces, Ramos was looked upon as the champion of the aggrieved. Those officers who were blocked or bypassed in promotion took their cases to Ramos. Complaints of the common soldiers—poor pay, inadequate training, neglect, abuse, lack of supplies and equipment—found their way up the chain of command to Ramos. In the rivalry between Ver on the one hand and Enrile and Ramos on the other, Marcos and the First Lady overwhelmingly favored Ver. On one occasion Imelda remarked, "Nothing bad will ever happen to the President and me; General Ver will not let it happen." Such was her blind faith!

It will be difficult for the military to regain the respect it lost as enforcer of the martial law system under Marcos. The AFP had to implement all laws, decrees, orders, and regulations issued by the President. It had to collect the firearms and enforce the curfew. It had to set up the military tribunals empowered to judge civilian as well as military personnel in all cases of alleged subversion, sedition, rebellion, or espionage. It had to carry out the hated presidential commitment orders and the preventive action detention decrees.

When martial law was declared in 1972, military personnel were ordered to arrest Benigno Aquino, Salonga, Diokno, and a host of other public figures. Soldiers, under orders, detained between 60,000 and 75,000 suspected subversives and applied the strong-arm methods associated with salvaging, kidnapping, and torture. The nuns in Task Force Detainees, an official group within the Catholic Church, claimed they had documentation on 1,451 salvaging cases and 411 disappearances between 1975 and 1983. Soldiers were called upon to use tear gas to break up rallies, strikes, and peaceful demonstrations. They were under orders to man the tanks that were stopped on EDSA Boulevard in Manila by "People Power." It was not very pleasant to do a "dog's dirty work for a dog's pay of $40 per month."

Marcos further diluted the professionalism of the military by projecting the officer corps into many civilian aspects of Philippine society. Retired military personnel were placed in key government positions. They managed many military-related industries: shipping lines, railways, civil aviation, and government insurance. They ran the postal service, prisons, public housing, and public utilities. They took excellent jobs in government research organizations and economic planning councils. Some served as judges, ambassadors, bankers, or heads of corporations. More than 300 senior-grade officers were sent abroad every year for graduate education and upon retirement were absorbed into the civil service or the private sector.

Their experience in engineering and construction thrust them into the forefront in national development. They continued to build bridges, roads, schools, irrigation dikes, and dams, but they also reforested thousands of acres of land, provided relief for disaster victims, and offered free medical and dental services to the poor. As presidential officers for regional development, 70 percent of whom were military, they were at the service of the first lady for implementing the projects of her Ministry of Human Development. In the city of Manila, the army engineers were obliged to hop to it when she called for lightning completion of a culture center, a luxury hotel, a convention center, or a guest house for the papal visit.

The military increased in power and in access to power, taking local command in the provinces. For the local politician who could once suggest appointments or call Malacañang and get a response, it became important to know somebody at military headquarters rather than someone in city hall.

It was inevitable that as the military expanded its political and economic activities, it would succumb to the "conspicuous consumption" aspect of the life of the privileged. Some generals lived in the finest homes, amassed great wealth, and enjoyed the protection of Malacañang. They spread out into the lucrative rackets of protecting prostitutes, pimps, and gamblers. One retired general in Central Luzon was said to own "a hauling business, three mansions, two subdivisions, a 50-door apartment complex, a cattle ranch, a wine store and pawn shop, vast real estate holdings in California, a fleet of expensive cars, a cache of high-powered guns, huge dollar deposits here and abroad, and many more trappings of ill-gotten wealth that would really boggle one's imagination." The generals were practically immune to the law; they were without competition when they went into business. More than half were "overstaying," meaning they were allowed to continue on active duty beyond normal retirement.

With no Congress to check on the commander-in-chief and no strident media to criticize military excesses, the decent elements within the armed forces decided to reform themselves. Early in 1985 U.S. Assistant Secretary of Defense Richard Armitage reminded Americans that the AFP had a corps of patriotic officers for whom the public welfare was a priority and who had a wealth of knowledge on how to combat insurgency. Alarmed by sagging morale and the stark contrast between the bacchanalian style of life in Manila and the hard life of the common soldiers in the combat zones, they dedicated themselves to the restoration of discipline, integrity, and professionalism in the armed forces.

A loosely organized effort to attain these goals was evident at the March 1985 graduation exercises of the Philippine Military Academy (the West Point of the Philippines). A group of officers wore T-shirts with the slogan "We Belong" printed on the front. They belonged to the incipient Reform the Armed Forces Movement (RAM), whose role in the overthrow of Marcos has already been described. They announced as their goal "fair-minded armed forces in the service of the country and the people." Toward that end they wanted better pay and better treatment, removal of the overstaying generals, promotions based on merit, better equipment and better training, rotation of troops to combat zones, and the weeding-out of corruption.

While maintaining a low profile and keeping out of the limelight, RAM grew to involve perhaps 1,500 of 13,500 officers. Enrile and Ramos encouraged them. Colonel Irwin Ver tried to join but was rejected. Marcos actually received their representatives in May 1985, listened to them, and then dismissed them with the observation that "they were airing the usual soldier gripes." In the words of one of their leaders, "We were wooed like hell from right and left, but we were determined to be independent." He continued, "We are not politically motivated, we do not want a coup d'etat, we do not want to be involved in a power struggle; all we seek are reforms in the military."

Whatever their goals and desires, they were not "a cooked-up CIA scheme," as the communists charged. Inspired and led by Enrile, they plotted to get rid of Marcos and might well have launched a coup of their own had not the people's revolution intervened.

As long as the armed forces were regarded as the tools of Marcos, the Manila populace feared the consequences of a possible military coup. The city was rife with rumors about "operation mad dog," which was the code name for the mass killings that were foreseen if and when the military were to take over in Malacañang. These rumors were put to rest when most of the military teamed up with their Filipino brothers and sisters in toppling Marcos from power.

THE AQUINO
REVIVAL

The Aquino effort to preserve law and order is entirely different from that of Marcos. Scorning the ways of spooks and secret police, she is pledged to do away with abuse and to respect the rights of every citizen. No one appreciates more than she that the causes of social injustice must be removed if crimes of violence are to be reduced. Although she comes from a wealthy background, she empathizes with the plight of the poor. Whether her goals are determined by her personal character or her religious training, the issue of major concern in her entire economic program is the welfare of the impoverished masses. She argues that if men and women are relieved of hunger and pain, they are less likely to turn to crime.

With the elimination of martial law and the rapid dismemberment of the authoritarian law-enforcement apparatus, crimes of violence inevitably escalated. The Filipino inclination to "fight it out" rather than "argue it out" reasserted itself. Newly emerged political leaders surrounded themselves with armed security guards prone to transform the most trivial quarrels into ordeals of knives or pistols. Sales of small arms and machine guns soared as gangs and goons terrorized the countryside and the city streets. Not a day passed without a dozen killings reported in the local press. Until the situation improves foreign investors and tourists will shy away from the Philippines, and the land will know no peace.

In the long run the preservation of law and order depends upon the entire nation and not on the president and her administration alone—and this Cory knows. All the decrees and laws of her government will be ineffective unless the people rectify their behavior and work to strengthen their weakened institutions. The family, church, schools, and local leaders must reassume their traditional roles as the sustainers of law and order and the stabilizers of Philippine society.

The difficulty is that the short-range law-and-order situation is too critical to wait for long-range factors to become operative. Cory knows that her government enjoys popular support, that people are grateful for their newfound freedom. Those who espouse the centrist path to internal stability look to her to take action now to refashion and reform the peacekeeping agencies—the police and the military—to protect the law-abiding populace from the extremists on the right or left who threaten to tear Philippine society to shreds.

Aware that the peacekeeping function of the government is the prime responsibility of the armed forces, President Aquino made the creation of a new image for her "defenders of democracy" her first priority. She added the word *New* to the official designation of the Armed Forces of the Philippines. Her perception of reforms most urgently required in the military establishment included a redefinition of the respective roles to be played by police and professional soldiers, reorganization of institutional structures, and the injection of a new spirit of integrity and professional pride. Intent on preserving the best of military traditions in the Philippines, she set to work to wipe out the evils to which the armed forces under Marcos had fallen prey. Her objective was to restore the confidence of the people in the military and to return it to its honored place in Philippine society.

The new president was conscious of her obligation to the military for their role in precipitating the revolution that put her in power. Although she could not accept Enrile's claim that he was entitled to full partnership in her government—which, according to him, was nothing more than a coalition between herself and the military—

President Aquino with Chief of Staff General Fidel Ramos, reviewing the troops prior to her visit to the United States.

she acknowledged her debt of gratitude by appointing him minister of defense. General Ramos's reward was to become chief of staff.

Once in office, the new president gave immediate attention to the agencies of law enforcement—the police and the military—initiating organizational changes in the makeup of the Integrated National Police, the Philippine Constabulary, and the Armed Forces of the Philippines (AFP)—changes that could only become effective with the passage of time. She ordered the separation of the police and the military and began the process of returning at least a part of the police functions to the local authorities. As an immediate measure to tighten discipline among the police, she ordered punishment for wrongdoers and rewards for meritorious performance of duty.

Affirming her respect for the military as the guardian of Philippine democracy, she aimed to restore to it the prestige it had enjoyed under Magsaysay. In a speech to the graduating class of the Philippine Military Academy in 1986, she reminded her listeners that "the revolution began with a bullet—a bullet fired by a soldier into the head of my husband" but told them that she does not hold this against the entire military establishment, only against its misguided elements. As General Ramos put it, "Any large organization has its share of scalawags, and we have less than 2 percent in the AFP." Herself one of the victims of military abuse, she urged the people to join her in forgiving and forgetting.

President Aquino's instructions to the Presidential Commission on Human Rights (PCHR) and the Anti-Graft and Corrupt Practices Board of the AFP were to "go after the scalawags." Her appointees to the PCHR included the impeccable Jose Diokno as chairman, assisted by a former justice of the Supreme Court, the judge advocate of the New Armed Forces, a law professor from the University of the Philippines, a Catholic sister who kept the list of detainees for Amnesty International, the minister of justice, and her two personal representatives, the human rights lawyers Joker Arroyo and Rene Saguisag. They were assigned to clean up abuses by the military, punish the culprits, and compensate the victims. Prime targets were General Ver's intelligence apparatus and the major service commanders, who had become "chief clerks within a command system that led to a Pontius Pilate washing of hands about human rights abuses."

Two straight-as-a-stick, old-time generals, Manuel Flores and Luis Villareal, were named to head the Anti-Graft and Corrupt Practices Board. To spend a morning with them, as I did, is to develop the greatest confidence in their integrity. They had files on some 600 military men identified with acts of corruption, of which 44 were of star rank and 26 others were field-grade officers. They were determined to find out why troops in the field were short of ammunition, water containers, jungle packs, and combat boots, and to see that the guilty were punished. They promised that there would be no witch-hunting, and no trial by publicity, but neither would there be a white-wash. They hoped that their mandate would allow them to look into irregularities in the U.S. military assistance program. They simply could not understand why the Philippine military was allowed to buy nineteen Sikorsky helicopters with $63 million in Pentagon funds. The choppers, useless for military purposes, were used primarily for VIP transport and standby emergency lift capability. "What that means," according to one military officer, is that "Marcos and Ver bought the choppers to save their asses if everything goes to hell."

Working through Enrile, the consummate politician, and Ramos, the low-key professional soldier, Cory stepped up the process of reform that was so urgently needed. She revamped the command structure and put new blood in the top posts. In her first hundred days, she removed more than half of the overstaying generals, replaced 115 of the higher ranking officers with younger men, and transferred many of the "fat cats" in the Presidential Security Command to combat duty in the provinces. The best tanks, jeeps, and personnel carriers—which had been hoarded in Manila—were sent to fighting zones. To toughen up her men, she instituted a rigorous retraining program and ordered her procurement team to lay off the high-tech stuff and to acquire supplies and equipment that would enable the AFP to move, to communicate, and to shoot. She initiated an indoctrination program on value formation. Ultimately, she wanted all her soldiers to attend seminars designed to transform them into "God-centered, people-oriented, nation-focused "defenders of democracy."

President Aquino's reforms tended further to divide the military. While some of the best known generals were put under house arrest, hundreds of soldiers went AWOL. The hard-bitten among the military were cynical about the burst of morality that Cory symbolized. They resented the "saints" in the civil government prying into their personal affairs. They objected to "communists" and "pinkos" holding high offices in the new administration. Having suffered many casualties in the field, they saw no sense in a cease-fire and amnesty for their former enemies, the NPA.

The Marcos men remaining in the armed forces and their accomplices among the local officials grew angrier as "dubious characters" swelled the ranks of the hastily appointed OICs. Many local areas seethed. A newly appointed governor in Mindanao arrived at his office and read the sign on his door, "Welcome, and congratulations on your new assignment. However, if you ever sit in my chair I will kill you." Morale declined because promised pay raises were not forthcoming. Thousands of ex-police and unattached CHDF, uncertain about their future, became guns-for-hire. Warlords had no trouble in finding as many recruits as they could pay for.

With the rising popular demand for the reopening of the Aquino assassination case, a further loss in prestige for the military seemed inevitable. A commission of the Supreme Court recommended that the previous proceedings be declared a mistrial because "the evidence showed clearly that Marcos was personally responsible for suppression of vital evidence, harassment of witnesses, coaching of defense counsels, and even for the very decision rendered in the case." The commission noted that during the trial two prosecution witnesses disappeared and were now feared dead. A Japanese journalist who accompanied Aquino on the plane was shot at during a later visit to Manila; and a woman who said she actually saw a soldier kill Aquino was threatened, harassed, and offered bribes to keep her from testifying. The retrial of the twenty-five military people, including General Ver, was bound to further weaken the military, already severely handicapped in its campaigns against the MNLF and the NPA.

As long as Enrile was minister of defense, he was a thorn in the flesh of the administration. With a power base in his home province and many devotees among the soldiers in the ranks, he presumed to speak for the military. No one, however, who had suffered at his hands—and there were many—was willing to accept him as the instrument for restoring the military to a high place of dignity and respect in Philippine society. As minister of defense, his conduct was totally unmilitary. He openly defied the president, his commander-in-chief, and clashed with his chief of staff in the operational control of the troops. In a comic opera incident in early July—popularly billed as a military coup—Marcos's vice-presidential running mate, Senator Arturo Tolentino, supported by rebel soldiers, occupied the famous Manila Hotel, where he proclaimed himself president of the Philippines. When government troops moved into position around the hotel to take him into custody an armed clash seemed imminent. After two days of "discussions," Tolentino was persuaded to give up. Enrile emerged as the man of the hour. As leader of the government forces, he was credited with avoiding bloodshed. On the other hand, it was noted that the rebels also accepted him as their commander. He ordered them back to the barracks, where he punished them by ordering them to do thirty extra pushups.

In the succeeding months Manila was kept on edge with rumors of pending coups, allegedly to be masterminded by Enrile—backed by Marcos money—and executed by army units fed up with Cory's soft-on-communist policies. General Ramos repeatedly put the armed forces on red alert, especially when the president was absent—visiting the United States in September and Japan in October. On her return from Japan, assured of the backing of General Ramos and the United States, she fired Enrile and replaced him with General Rafael "Rocky" Ileto.

General Ileto, the new minister of defense, is a West Point graduate, class of 1943, and a veteran of World War II in the Southwest Pacific.

Under Magsaysay in the 1950s he organized and commanded the swift-striking, small-unit ranger teams that were successful in putting down the Huks. Staying clear of politics, he then earned a law degree at the University of Manila. After serving as a military attaché in Laos and Vietnam, Ileto returned to the Philippines to become operations chief of the National Intelligence Coordinating Agency (NICA). He rose rapidly in the military to the position of commanding general of the Northern Luzon region, assistant chief of staff for intelligence, and then commanding general of the Philippine army. Because he opposed Marcos's proclamation of martial law, he was cashiered from the armed forces and sent as ambassador first to Tehran and then to Bangkok, where he carefully observed methods of countering rebellion and insurgency.

Back again in his home country at the critical time of the People's Revolution, he offered to act as intermediary between General Ver and the Enrile-Ramos forces should his services be needed. When President Aquino moved into the presidency, she chose him to be her deputy minister of defense. When Enrile departed, Ileto simply moved up to fill the vacancy. Contrasting with Enrile's flamboyance, Ileto is cool, forceful, and soft-spoken. Unlike Enrile, regarded by many as a *sip sip* (fake) militarist, Ileto is universally respected as a true professional soldier.

THE COMPLEXITY OF
THE CHALLENGE

In taking charge of the ministry of defense, Ileto inherited an administrative muddle. The armed forces were in disarray. Every member of the military was uncertain about his own status and his future. Wholesale discharges and reassignments had taken their toll on morale. No one knew which officers were "in" and which were "out" and serious questions were raised as to whether the administration would be able to stay on top of the rivalries and schisms that wracked the military organization. Many of the older officers still doubted the patriotism of the We Belong reformers; the graduates of the Philippine Military Academy regarded the products of the ROTC as outsiders; and the remaining Ilocano Marcos appointees resented being pushed aside by the up and coming officers from the other provinces. The unity of the military was completely shattered by open and secret factions with names like RAM, El Diablo Guardian Foundation, and Guardian Brotherhood. The genuine nucleus of dedicated professionals hated to see the proliferation of cliques with loyalties to particular individuals—a local political leader, the minister of defense, the chief of staff, or even the president herself. The oath of the soldier was to protect the state and the people—not any particular wielder of power within it.

The replacement of Enrile by Ileto did not heal the breach between the civil authorities and the military, nor end the factionalism in the disgruntled army. The troubles in the military establishment reduced its reputation to a new low, which culminated in the incidents known as the Mendiola Massacre and the Mutiny at Channel 7, both of which took place just before the plebiscite on the constitution.

On January 22, 1987, about 10,000 peasants from Central Luzon belonging to the *Kilusang Mabubukid ng Pilipinas* (KMP) or Movement of Filipino Farmers, having tried without success to bring their demands for land reform to the personal attention of President Aquino, organized a protest march to the gates of Malacañang. When they reached Mendiola Bridge in front of the palace they were met by a hail of bullets from marines acting as riot police. Twelve were killed and many injured. The officers in command claimed that communists planted among the protesters fired first. The media crucified Cory and the military for killing the poorest of the poor in cold blood. Cory herself was not even in Manila on the day of the "massacre," but as commander-in-chief she had to bear the public's wrath. One paper declared, "She is worse than Marcos; her image is damaged beyond repair" and "Stained with blood, her government will never be the same again." Two officers considered responsible for the unfortunate incident were placed on administrative leave pending the report of a citizens' investigating committee.

Without rescuing the military from condemnation, Cory deftly salvaged her own reputation. Sunday, January 25, was her 54th birthday. To celebrate the event, another group of protesters lined up twelve coffins at the site of the "massacre" and organized another rally and march to the palace. This time Cory was home and she handled the crowd in her own way. Ignoring security, she dismissed the military completely. She invited the leaders personally to discuss their problems with her. Instead of marines, a human chain joined by her cabinet officers and senior staff met the marchers and peacefully diverted them down a side street. To a certain extent Cory was absolved from guilt in the Mendiola tragedy, but the military remained under a cloud.

The mutiny at Channel 7 also had the effect of improving the image of Cory at the expense of the military. On Monday morning, January 26, Manila awoke to the news that rebellious army units backed by pro-Marcos civilians (including movie actresses) occupied the premises of the TV channel 7–Radio Station DZBB complex, while other rebel troops stormed the Philippine Air Force headquarters at the Villamor Air Station, near the Manila International Airport and the armory at Sangley Point Air Station, taking the commanding general and his deputy as hostages. As soon as the news was confirmed, President Cory went on nationwide TV to announce a "get tough" policy. She said: "When in the past they went to the Manila Hotel, we forgave them. But now we can no longer allow this foolishness and troublemaking, so they now have to face our courts." She continued, "The full force of the law will be applied to everyone, civilian and military, who is implicated in this crime. I have ordered their arrest and detention. There is a time for reconciliation and a time for justice and retribution. That time has come."

Whether it was her fault, or the fault of General Ramos, the tough policy was not implemented. The scenes at Villamor and Sangley

The military confronting the crowds at Mendiola Bridge, just prior to the February 2, 1987 plebiscite on the Constitution. A dozen civilians were killed in these demonstrations.

A human chain, including President Aquino's cabinet officers and senior staff, peacefully diverted from Malacañang marchers protesting the killings at Mendiola Bridge.

Point were quickly pacified, but the drama at Channel 7 dragged on for three days. The rebels there were given an ultimatum, "Leave the premises or you will be attacked." They ignored the warning, but nothing happened. Back at military headquarters, some sixty middle-rank officers identified with the RAM pleaded with Ramos and Ileto not to spill blood. The next day Ramos decided to talk with the rebels, who chose one of their number, Col. Oscar Canlas, to be their spokesman. For two hours the country was treated on national TV to the demeaning spectacle of the chief of staff haranguing with an officer very much his junior in what appeared to be a schoolboy debate. The general told the colonel how naughty he was, and the colonel replied that everything the rebels did was only to stiffen the government's backbone in fighting the communists. At the end of the conversation, Canlas was not led off to prison in handcuffs but was escorted to a press conference, where he was received more like a hero than a mutineer.

The whole sorry performance further damaged the public image of the military. It was reported that the rebel officers involved in the episode were paid up to $3,000 and the enlisted men up to $100 each, presumably by Marcos or one of his cronies, for the parts they played. The coup, if it could be called that, was linked up with a Marcos effort to charter a Boeing 707 from Honolulu and return to the Philippines in time to upset the scheduled plebiscite. Some 13 officers and 359 enlisted men were held for later trial on charges ranging from mutiny to conduct unbecoming an officer. Further orders were issued for the arrest of one general, two colonels, and a major suspected of long-term plotting, but they disappeared into the hills before the orders could be carried out.

As the differences between the president and her senior military officers sharpened, public opinion supported Cory far more than Ramos and Ileto. As one columnist wrote, "All Canlas's talk of defending and upholding democracy is sham and utterly hypo-critical. The military runs on one key element, discipline, and the army will be divided as long as discipline is not enforced. Colonel Canlas should have been courtmartialed, and not welcomed back with open arms and a hot breakfast." The public wanted Cory to be tough on the military, just as the military wanted Cory to be tough on the communists.

The new constitution offered no contribution to smoothing the relations between civilian authorities and the military. It merely affirmed that "civilian authority is at all times supreme over the military" and that "the Armed Forces of the Philippines is the protector of the people and the State." Under the General Provisions, it provides that "the State shall strengthen the patriotic spirit and national conscious-ness of the military, and respect for people's rights in the performance of their duty." The military did not like the constitution, and it is estimated that they voted 3 to 2 against it.

The military has more complaints against the president than it has against the constitution. Many soldiers of all ranks and descriptions do not like the idea of a woman as their commander-in-chief. They think she has no fundamental sympathy with their calling, has little appreciation of their hardships and deprivations, and tends to treat them as second-class citizens. They have reservations about her per-formance as president. In their view, she has too many anti-military leftwingers in her cabinet and does not sufficiently heed her military advisers. Pursuing her policy of reconciliation, she was quick to for-give the communists but allows her anti-graft committee and Presi-dential Commission of Good Government to hound the military.

They claim that she alone is responsible for the good name and effective performance of the armed forces and should not try to shift her responsibilities as commander-in-chief to her military staff.

As Cory enters the post-constitutional stage of her administration, her command of the military may emerge as the most vulnerable aspect of her program for maintaining law and order. Having been pampered for so long, the military will not easily surrender its privileges and power. Many in the Philippines still fear the possibility of a military coup such as occurred in its neighbor nations, Indonesia and Thailand. Actually, however, their situation is entirely different. The minute one talks about a military coup in the Philippines, the inevitable question arises, "What military?" A world of difference separates the combat-ready units—the professional soldiers—from the politically oriented, technically trained officers who are more at home in Manila than in the provinces. The PC, INP, and CHDF are all grouped under the rubric "military" but their loyalties and capabilities are as diverse as their places of origin. Military units could easily take over government buildings and kill government officials, but thay have neither the resources nor the personnel to run the country.

With all its faults, the military is still one of the strongest pillars of Philippine society. No matter how divided within itself, the military quickly closes ranks when attacked by an outsider. Soldiers are extremely reluctant to harm one another or to fire on their own. Although the military has no tradition of governing, it has no lack of confidence in its ability to govern. The military did not hesitate to defy Marcos and would not hesitate to move against Cory if convinced that she were not equal to her job. Having known their moments of glory in World War II and in Magsaysay's day, they would like to have such moments again.

It is perfectly obvious that the Filipinos must get their military house in order. President Aquino's first responsibility is to carry out the reforms that will transform the fragmented military into an effective fighting machine. Only then will it be able to join with the people and the civilian authorities in the common struggle to bring about political stability and to settle the problems of the Muslims and the communist insurgents.

6

"We Moros want what is ours,
but we will not
get down on our knees to beg for peace."

Muslim leader Nur Misuari, negotiating
with a Philippine government delegation

THE
MORO
REBELLION

In Mindanao, the Aquino administration inherited a condition of near anarchy. Mindanao is the large island in the southern Philippines flanked by the Sulu Archipelago, Palawan, and two smaller islands, Basilan and Tawi Tawi. These islands are inhabited by distinct tribes—Tausug, Maguindanao, Maranao, Yakan, Samal, and several other minor ones—whose ancestors were established there long before Magellan and the Spanish conquistadores arrived. They pursued traditional ways of life—fishing, farming, and fighting each other—and in various ways, and to varying degrees, accepted the religion of Islam. They were at the extreme end of the eastward Muslim expansion that reached the Philippines from India through neighboring Indonesia.

For four hundred years the Catholic Spanish fought the Muslim "infidels," whom they dubbed *Moros*, because to them they were the same breed as the Moors they fought back home. As for the Moros, the islands were their homes; they would rather die than surrender to the alien invaders. There was no blending of cultures, no intermarriage, and no Moro *mestizo* class. The Spanish did not make a cadastral survey such as they had made in Luzon and the Visayas, which would have confirmed ownership and set the limits of private property of the southern Philippines. It was death by *kris*, or crossbow, for Spanish soldiers in Moroland who dared to venture beyond the bounds of their coastal garrisons. The Catholic Church established itself only where its communicants could be adequately defended. When the Spanish finally left the Philippines, the Muslim way of life was as tradition bound as it had been when they arrived.

When the religiously tolerant Americans succeeded the Catholic Spanish, the Moros continued the fight to preserve their own religion, their institutions, and their customs. They were never conquered, but they were deeply influenced by the impact of American rule and the American philosophy of an open society, rugged individualism, and public education as the avenue to a better future. Local schools with American teachers were established and opened to Moro children, thus exposing them to ideas other than the writings of the Koran. Scholarships enabled the best and the brightest to go on to the University of the Philippines so that, inevitably, an increasing number of educated Moros began to fraternize with their Christian Filipino counterparts.

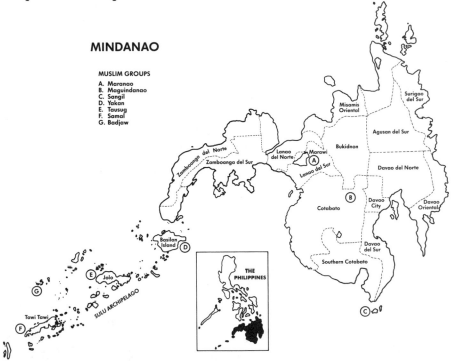

MINDANAO

MUSLIM GROUPS
A. Maranao
B. Maguindanao
C. Sangil
D. Yakan
E. Tausug
F. Samal
G. Badjaw

Anticipating quick independence for the Philippines, as provided in the Jones Act of 1916, the Americans pursued an active national development policy for their colony, taking full advantage of the economic potential of resource-rich, underdeveloped Mindanao. The empty spaces of Mindanao looked as attractive to heavily populated Luzon and the Visayas as the Far West in the United States had looked to the Eastern Seaboard. In 1920, as soon as the exigencies of World War I permitted, a Bureau of Non-Christian Tribes was set up in the Philippine Department of the Interior under the control of the Philippine Legislature. Filipinos in the north were encouraged to migrate south and were given title to the land on which they settled. Rich and influential Filipinos were, at the same time, given huge grants of unoccupied, untilled "public" lands for logging or cattle ranches. Multinationals from Japan or the United States were given grants large enough for abaca (Manila hemp), bananas, or pineapples, but not large enough for rubber—which Ford, Firestone, and Edison would have liked to develop.

At the same time, Muslim clan leaders were invited to apply for legal title to lands they had assumed to be theirs for centuries. The Muslim community split. Some leaders, sensing new opportunities for profit, accepted; others indignantly rejected the invitation. As the population of Mindanao increased, more government jobs were opened, both for favored Filipinos and for trained Muslims. A new Muslim elite, based on wealth and political influence, was being born. As the old line *datus* (sultans) and Muslim teachers became aware of this rising challenge to their traditional leadership, they made clear to the Americans their preference to remain under American rule rather than to become a submerged minority in a newly independent Philippine nation.

Their fears were justified; when the Filipinos, as Catholic as the Spanish and less tolerant than the Americans, regained their independence, they tightened the screws on Moroland. Backed by the Philippine constabulary, they applied Philippine law as opposed to Muslim custom. The differences were most marked in matters of polygamous marriages, legitimacy of children, inheritance, status of women, and property rights. In political disputes, Muslims could expect no sympathy from Christian officials. Only as a last resort would a Muslim take his case to a government office or a court of law.

Moro-Filipino antagonisms were accentuated as the crowded north sent more of its excess population to the south. In the mid-1950s, President Magsaysay sought to ease the causes of agrarian discontent in Luzon by giving land grants to ex-Huks and resettling them in Mindanao. He underestimated the trouble he was building up in the south. On the surface, it appeared that all of Mindanao was the richer because of increased immigration. In reality, native Muslims were denied the prosperity enjoyed by the Christian newcomers. By 1983, some 80 percent of Mindanao's 10 million people were non-Muslim. Only two percent of Davao, the largest city in the south and the third largest city in the Philippines, were Muslims. Native Muslims had been overrun by the homesteading Christians in much the same way that the American Indians were displaced by trespassing settlers.

THE MARCOS POLICIES

When Marcos became president, western Mindanao was already a tinderbox. Armed gangs of Muslims, with names like "black-shirts" in Cotabato and "barracudas" in Lanao, took the law into their own hands. Engaging in the kidnapping and killing of Christians, they roamed at will. Gangs of renegade Christians, variously called Rizal Christians, Rock Christs, *Ilagas* (rats), or Lost Commands, re-taliated against the Muslims with equal barbarity. The situation was beyond the control of law.

In 1968 the tinderbox burst into flame. Marcos recruited some two hundred Moros, mostly Tausugs from Jolo, to train in secrecy on the island of Corregidor for jungle survival, infiltration, sabotage, and assassination, presumably in preparation for a move against the neighboring state of Sabah on the Malaysian segment of the island of Borneo. The project was given the code name of *Jabidah*. Unpaid and mistreated by their Filipino officers, the Moros mutinied. They were rounded up and massacred. Only one Moro managed to escape to tell his frightful tale to the world.

Muslims in the Philippines and throughout the world were en-raged. A Muslim Independence Movement (MIM) arose. Its leaders demanded a separate state, to be called *Minsupala* and to comprise the major portions of Mindanao, the Sulu archipelago, and Palawan. They knew very well that a separate state was an impossibility, that Philippine nationalism was too strong, and that the Muslims had become a minority in their own homeland. Nevertheless, they demanded an independent separate state—implying secession from the Republic of the Philippines as their ideal.

Marcos ordered the MIM to disband and sent military reinforcements to carry out his orders. The fighting and the killings increased. Schools were closed, the economy disrupted, and thousands of refugees were forced to abandon their homes. The Moro Rebellion provided Marcos with one of his major justifications for imposing martial law. No sooner had he done so (in 1972) than he ordered the immediate collection of guns from all civilians, including the Moros. For the Moros, the right to bear arms is sanctioned by the Koran and therefore sacred. Guns not only mean their livelihood; they are also their pride and joy, the symbol of their *macho*, and the sole weapon on which they can rely to protect their most precious possession, the Muslim way of life. They simply refused to obey the Marcos order.

Resistance became organized in Lanao, Cotabato, and Zamboanga (all in western Mindanao), and in Tawi Tawi, Basilan, and the Sulu archipelago. The Moros formed the Moro National Liberation Front (MNLF), with the Bangsa Moro Army (BMA) as its military arm. Enjoying the sympathy of the entire Muslim world, the Moros received aid from Khadafi and weapons from various sources channeled through neighboring Sabah, Malaysia. For more than two years the fighting raged. The Moros put 30,000 rebels in the field against 50,000 government troops—some 75 to 80 percent of the entire combat strength of the AFP. Casualties were heavy and the destruction appalling. More than 100,000 Muslims may have died and 200,000 been driven away from their homes as refugees. In the course of incessant shelling and bombing by government forces, the old cities of Jolo and Marawi were completely razed.

As war weariness settled on both sides, Marcos used the "carrot" as well as the "stick" to cope with the rebels. He played one Moro leader against another, offering amnesty, jobs, and money to those who would join him. He persuaded Malaysia and Libya to cut down the flow of arms to the rebels and sought the assistance of Khadafi and the Organization of the Islamic Conference in working out a truce arrangement.

In the meantime, although Marcos diverted more development assistance to Mindanao, the Moros complained that they were left out of its benefits. High visibility projects like hydroelectric power plants, shipbuilding, and a steel complex were wonderful for the cronies but provided nothing for the Muslims. Port improvement, roads, dams, rural electrification, and cheap lands were fine for the pineapple and banana plantations of the foreign multinationals, but they did not alleviate the hardships of the Moros, who had to live on their coconuts, upland rice, root crops, and fish. Between 1966 and 1976, in spite of the chaos and near-anarchy, nearly 700,000 hectares of land were allotted to newcomers, and more than three million Christian settlers trekked into Mindanao.

Talks in Tripoli in 1976 involving the MNLF, Mrs. Marcos (representing the Philippine government), Khadafi, and representatives of the Organization of the Islamic Conference produced an agreement on cease-fire and tentative terms for a peace settlement. The cease-fire went into effect immediately, while negotiations continued to implement the terms of peace. The Tripoli Agreement made no reference to the possibility of a separate, independent Muslim state. On the contrary, it provided for autonomy in thirteen provinces. The autonomy was to include Muslim courts, a legislative assembly and executive council, an autonomous administrative system, special regional security forces, and representation in the central government; control over education, finance, and the economic system; and the right to a reasonable percentage of the revenues of mines and minerals. The central government was to maintain responsibility for foreign policy and national defense. The role of the MNLF Forces and the AFP, and the relationships between structures and policies of the autonomous region and the central government, were to be discussed later.

Once the Tripoli Agreement was signed, Marcos proceeded to dismantle it. He held a plebiscite in the thirteen provinces, in effect asking the voters to choose between a merger into a single autonomous unit, as proposed by the Tripoli Agreement, or to continue the existing system of one regional government at Cotabato and another at Zamboanga, both under the control of the Philippine central government. Since the majority Christians as well as the minority Muslims were allowed to vote, the proposal for the merger was overwhelmingly rejected. In October 1977, the cease-fire broke down and the MNLF embarked on a course that was progressively downhill.

The Muslim cause lost a great deal of its outside support due to the sharp dissension within the Arab world community. Libya, Iran, and Syria approved the revolutionary qualities they saw in the MNLF; Egypt and the Saudis were less interested in revolution than in strengthening the religious orthodoxy of the Muslims within the

Philippine nation-state. There was no way to get all Arabs interested in a possible holy war in the Philippines. Khadafi lost interest in the Philippines; Khomeini could not let Philippine problems divert his interest from Iran's war with Iraq; and the Organization for the Islamic Conference was not inclined to protest the Marcos announcement that no foreign entity would in the future be permitted to interfere in strictly internal Philippine affairs.

The leadership of the MNLF fell apart. Before Tripoli, the accepted leader was Nur Misuari, a Tausug, who had become a Marxist revolutionary while studying at the University of the Philippines. Forced to live in exile like the other Moro leaders, he chose Libya, where he benefited from the support of Khadafi and Khomeini. He had to suffer the consequences of his diplomatic defeat at Tripoli. He was accused by opponents within the MNLF of being far more interested in a revolutionary victory than in the preservation of Muslim orthodoxy. Thwarted in his effort to achieve autonomy within the Philippine national framework, he resumed his campaign for an independent Bangsa Moro Republic. He was opposed by Hashim Salamat, a Maguindanao tribal leader and conservative graduate of Cairo University in Egypt. Salamat felt that Misuari was "all wind," that he had deserted the fighting troops in the field. Salamat set up a "Moro Islamic Liberation Front" with headquarters in Karachi. He was willing to settle for autonomy, as was another dissident faction within the MNLF known as the Reform Group and headed by Dimas Pundato, a Maranao tribesman, with headquarters in Sabah.

Just before the assassination of Ninoy Aquino in 1983, Secretary of Defense Enrile announced that he considered the Moro rebellion to be contained. He called attention to the divided leadership and to the attrition suffered by the Moro fighters. Only Nur Misuari wanted to continue the fighting; the other leaders were disposed to make whatever deals they could for the benefit of themselves and their followers.

AQUINO AND
THE MOROS

When Marcos left office, every single Moro leader disagreed with Enrile's assessment that the Moro rebellion was effectively contained. They insisted that the Moro cause was alive and the MNLF was still its champion. It claimed a force of 15,000 fighters, 80 percent of them below age twenty, with 12,000 reserves. Its mass base was intact. It could no longer strike in battalion strength, but its guerrilla hit-and-run tactics tied down large numbers of government forces that could have been usefully deployed elsewhere. The guerrilla forces had access to arms and they had training camps in Libya, Syria, and Sabah. Substantial financial support came from the 16,000 Muslims among the contract workers from the Philippines in the Middle East. Many MNLF cadres left the Philippines as legitimate workers, received secret military training abroad, and returned to the Philippines as Muslim commandos.

The MNLF insisted that its motivation was political, aiming only at eventual independence. Resorting to arms was a necessity not of its own choice. Accepted as a full-fledged member of the Organization of the Islamic Conference, with Nur Misuari as its recognized leader, it set up official missions in the name of the Bangsa Moro Republic in Libya and Syria. Disclaiming responsibility for extortions, kidnap-

"Butz" Aquino, brother of Ninoy Aquino, with Moslem leader Nur Misuari in Mindanao, representing the government in negotiations for peaceful settlement of divisive issues.

pings, and ambushes carried out by independent Moro groups, it disavowed responsibility for urban warfare in Zamboanga. The MNLF denied vehemently that it was a terrorist organization and declared that its armed forces would strike only at military targets.

The Moros—those inside the MNLF who opposed the leadership of Nur Misuari and those outside the MNLF who operated independently—also contributed to the unrest and violence throughout the southern Philippines. Local leaders defied the government to come and get them. Pirates and smugglers infested the seas. Kidnappers threatened the lives of tourists, teachers, nuns, and missionaries, whom they held for ransom. While the argument could be made that the Moro rebellion was losing its strength, its danger was magnified because of the parallel threat to stability seen in the rising power of the communist insurgents, spearheaded by the NPA.

When Ninoy Aquino was alive, he said that if he were elected president, Mindanao would be the first item on his agenda. It was essentially the same with his widow. Her program was to take advantage of every opportunity to negotiate with all the Moro factions. She understood that she would have to provide for returnees (those who could return to the government fold) or they would head back to the hills. She replaced the most obnoxious of the ex-Marcos puppets in Mindanao and tried to give Muslims a more visible role in local government. She accepted the fact that their demands would have to be taken into account. They wanted fewer Christian soldiers in their vicinity because "we are tired of generals who have enriched themselves in logging, smuggling, or trading in coffee, rubber and copra." They demanded an end to military abuses. They took the position that soldiers should be returned from checkpoints along the rural highways to their provincial headquarters, and that law and order in the countryside be made the responsibility of local Muslim police.

Such demands could not be granted in toto, but they had to be placed on the agenda for negotiation. Furthermore, the Muslims asked the central government for a clear-cut program for rehabilitation and reconstruction. They wanted help in building roads and dams, schools and mosques. They sought government assistance in finding employment for Muslims who wanted to work in the Middle East. They wanted help in diversifying the economy of their region, developing mines and industries as well as more plantations. They wanted a bigger share of tourist dollars.

For the Muslims it was important that with the advent of the Aquino administration they no longer had to continue their rebellion against the government. There was no need to fight for their rights. That they could argue their case while sitting around a conference table was a hopeful sign. Cory was aware of the high stakes in her dealings with all Muslims, not only the MNLF. Denial of their rights meant that they would continue to fight; talking with Muslim leaders would at least give peaceful coexistence a chance. Throughout the discussions, her principal objectives were to preserve national unity and to uphold the sovereignty of the national government. She also recognized the need for guaranteeing the rights of the minority. The deep hostility between the factions within the Muslim community complicated her problems.

Preliminary understandings were reached with the factions headed by Hashim Salamat and Dimas Pundatun. Realizing that a separate Muslim state was not obtainable, they limited their demands to autonomy and guarantees of minority rights. Being traditional and devout Muslims, they were more interested in religious welfare than in social revolution and consistently refused to cooperate with the godless communists. They feared, however, that Cory was too Catholic, too mesmerized by the Jesuits, who wield so much influence over the Christians in Mindanao. As dissidents within the MNLF, they were willing to enter into negotiations with the commanding general of the southern region, looking to a cease-fire pending a settlement of their grievances and their aspirations.

The most difficult problem for President Aquino was to lure Nur Misuari, acknowledged by most as the toughest leader of the MNLF, to the conference table. Nur Misuari is pro-Arab and anti-American. He curses the United States for having supplied arms to Marcos and brands President Reagan as "the mad dog of Israel." His faction is most clearly identified with the policy of continuing the Moro rebellion until the Bangsa Moro (Moro people) achieves its goal of a separate, independent Muslim homeland. His 8,000 guerillas, scattered throughout Southwest Mindanao and the Sulu archipelago, constitute a formidable fighting force, not merely an aggregation of farmers with guns. Not fanatical in their religion, but extremist in their desire for modernization and social revolution, they show no hesitancy in cooperating with the NPA.

Through her brother-in-law, Butz Aquino, Cory persuaded Nur Misuari to return to Mindanao after thirteen years in exile. He was guaranteed safe conduct and assured that for the sake of peace in

Mindanao, he himself could choose "who should sit beside him and who should sit behind him." Under a de facto cease-fire he met with President Aquino in a convent in Jolo in September 1986, and after a first round of discussions was given permission to travel freely throughout Muslim territory. Wherever he went, he rode in trucks loaned him by the government. He ate food provided by the government. Throughout his sojourn, the armed forces stayed in the background out of sight.

Thus Cory initiated a process that may take a long time to produce tangible results. The Moros are in no hurry to reach a settlement they might later regret. While she negotiates, and makes concessions to Nur Misuari, she risks undoing what she has accomplished with other factions. To deal with three at once requires skillful juggling. She feels, however, that she is best advised in concentrating on the MNLF. Both the government and the MNLF have engaged in sparring, each testing the other's capabilities and intentions. Although Nur Misuari is technically committed to the cause of Moro independence, it is Cory's hope and belief that he might be persuaded to settle for an autonomous region based on the terms of the defunct Tripoli agreement.

If she is to be criticized for lack of progress, it will have to be by those who disagree with her tactics. Vice-President Laurel thinks that she underestimates the element of foreign relations in the Moro problem, and that his ministry of foreign affairs should be given more responsibility. He objects to the extent to which Cory has informally involved her brother-in-law and her sister-in-law in such important matters of policy. She cannot, however, be faulted for lack of effort or understanding. She has appointed a presidential task force to deal with Mindanao and a minister of Muslim affairs in her cabinet.

Eventually, the Muslims will have to be granted some degree of autonomy. They do not want to be assimilated and they do not want to be a colony of Manila. They want their own schools, their own laws, and their own religious holidays. They want proportional representation in the central government and in the military. They want the power to tax and to run their own local government, leaving nothing to Manila but defense and foreign affairs. "We Moros want what is ours," they say, "but we will not get down on our knees to beg for peace." President Aquino's job is to continue the search for the kind of peace that will enable both sides to build a future based on mutual respect, trust, and goodwill.

7

"It is I who will decide
just what we do
in our country."

President Aquino to President Reagan

THE COMMUNIST INSURGENCY— THE NPA

Although Mindanao was the focal point of rebellion when Cory took office, the entire country was threatened by the rapid growth of the communist insurgency. The communists had extended their operations into practically every province in the Philippines, challenging the authority of government in the urban centers and smaller towns as well as in the rural areas. In a growing number of localities, law and order was collapsing, leaving the New People's Army (NPA) as the only governing agency. The severest test of the Aquino administration was—and still is—to establish stability where public order has broken down.

ORIGINS OF PHILIPPINE COMMUNISM

The communists have been active in the Philippines since 1930, when the Philippine economy was suffering the effects of the Great American Depression. A Moscow-oriented Filipino Communist Party, the *Partido Komunista ng Pilipinas* (PKP), joined the Socialist Party (also Marxist) in supporting peasant revolts in Luzon against the American regime. During World War II, the communists played a major role in the *Hukbalahap* (Huk) movement against the Japanese and—when the war ended—against the Philippine government. Magsaysay effectively destroyed the communist menace when he defeated the Huks in the field and, in an intelligence coup, arrested the entire communist politburo in Manila. For fourteen years (1954–1968) the PKP disappeared as an effective opposition force.

In 1968 the communist movement was resurrected. Young intellectual activists from the University of the Philippines, taking their cue from Maoist China rather than from Moscow, split off from the moribund PKP and organized a new Communist Party of the Philippines (CPP), with the NPA as its military arm. Depending upon themselves rather than on any foreign support, they followed the principle that "the armed struggle is the primary struggle we must wage." When Marcos proclaimed martial law in 1972, they took to the hills, establishing bases in the mountains of northern Luzon, in the Bicol region of southern Luzon, and on the island of Samar in the Visayas.

Life in the hills was cruel and survival would have to depend upon a support base. In the following year they organized the National Democratic Front (NDF) to carry out united front activities with the masses. Jose Marie Sison, the philosopher, was the founder-chairman of the CPP; his colleague, Bernabe Buscayno (alias Commander Dante), a militant young revolutionary, was the leader of the NPA; and Satur Ocampo, a former business editor of the most conservative newspaper in Manila, was appointed to head the NDF. All three were captured by Marcos intelligence officers in 1976 and 1977. Sison and Buscayno remained imprisoned until released by President Aquino; Ocampo escaped in 1985.

THE COMMUNIST PROGRAM AND POLICIES

The arrests of its leaders, combined with the difficulties of avoiding the government forces assigned to hunting them down, led to the adoption by the communists of a new CPP strategy of centralized planning and decentralized operations. Their basic program remains unchanged, even under the Aquino administration: They expect to advance through alternate stages of strategic *defense* (the stage they are in now) stalemate, and strategic *offense*. Their ultimate goal is to set up a "Democratic Peoples Republic of the Philippines." They still believe that they must pursue their objective by means of armed struggle, but if they succeed by peaceful methods and with a minimum of bloodshed, so much the better.

Being unequivocally opposed to imperialism, feudalism, and bureaucratic capitalism, the communists insist upon the immediate departure of the American military from the Philippine bases. They demand the cancellation of the mutual defense treaty and the termination of American military assistance. They will not tolerate American or Japanese multinationals in the Philippines, except on their own terms. They want their own army integrated into the AFP in the same way that the Communist Eighth Route Army was at one time incorporated into the nationalist armies of Chiang Kai-shek. As the price of reconciliation, they insist on representation in President Aquino's government. "We have had our February revolution," they say. "We are waiting for the October one."

Philosophically, the communists are no more compatible with Aquino than they were with Marcos. Although their stated aim is to reorient Philippine society along Marxist-Leninist lines, their domestic program is actually a cross between social reform, Marxist revolution, and extreme nationalism. The danger does not lie in the objectives they seek but rather in their willingness to resort to violence and terror to achieve their ends.

If feudal exploitation can be eliminated and the land problem can be solved, there is no reason, the communists argue, to resort to armed struggle. They are not concerned with the property rights of the landowners, but with justice for the peasants. Land must be made available for the growers, tillers, and agricultural workers. Such areas as logged-over lands and lands under pasture lease that are not actually being used by the dairy industry must be distributed. Usury must be outlawed and cheaper credit made available by rural banks. The peasants must be given the same opportunity for a better life as that enjoyed by the rest of Filipino society.

The CPP wants to free the Philippines from the plantation economy, which, as they see it, "would make us an agrarian paradise of oranges, mangoes, and shrimps." The Philippines, they argue, should have its own industrial base. The tools of production should be in the hands of the state, and the interests of the workers should be paramount. The entrepreneurial capacity of the Filipinos should be sufficiently developed to become dominant over the foreign sector in the Philippine economy.

In the party's struggle to survive and to extend its power, its program has been all but forgotten. While the program writers languished in jail, a tough new generation of leaders, including Rodolfo Salas and Rafael Baylosis, produced a blend of guerrilla warfare and united front tactics that humiliated and outlasted its enemy—the Marcos regime. The war between the government and the NPA was never a debate on Marxist dialectics; it was always a series of bloody battles fought on many fronts on many islands—Marcos and company versus the communist command and the united front, with millions of innocent victims tragically caught in the middle.

The organization chart for the communist insurgents places the politburo and the central committee at the top. They direct separate commissions for military, united front, propaganda, and mass movement activities established at national, regional, and island levels. The NDF is given responsibility for infiltrating and influencing such organizations as the Revolutionary Workers, Nationalist Women, Moro Revolutionaries, Basic Christian Communities, Task Force Detainees, Nationalist Peasants, Free Farmers, Nationalist Youth, and various teachers unions. Nothing escapes the communists' attention.

A close look at the NPA shows the average age as twenty, with some as young as twelve. They do not get their arms from China, Libya, or the Soviet Union, but from the United States. In Marcos's time, the Pentagon was the arsenal of the NPA, and Marcos himself was considered the chief transport and supply officer for the communists. First the arms were received by the AFP, and then the NPA got the arms through ambush, raids, or purchase on the black market. Father Balweg, the guerrilla leader in northern Luzon, once said to an American visitor, "Tell President Reagan to keep sending those guns because we can surely use them." Shortage of arms and ammunition is still the major factor in limiting the size of the NPA. It relies on hit-and-run strikes by small bands of forty to fifty to harass army patrols or to grab arms.

The prime political objective of guerrilla action is to overrun a *barangay* (village), to hold it, consolidate it, and develop it into a communist cell. Such cells have been established all over the Philippines. Party cadres follow the guerrillas, indoctrinate the local inhabitants in their own ideology, organize the men, women, and children into separate groups, and establish a shadow government. The new cell in turn develops its own militia and provides shelter and intelligence for the NPA. It also collects taxes, metes out instant justice, and raises the new recruits to carry on the fight against unpopular landlords and other counter-revolutionaries.

Life is precarious for those innocent civilians who happen to get caught in the crossfire between the NPA and the government forces. The NPA activists are not benign social reformers, nor are they, as Marcos called them, nothing but hoodlums and terrorists. They deny that they are another Khmer Rouge, claiming that "If we were as fiendish as they say we are, we would have been wiped out long ago." Nevertheless, it is tough on the villagers when either the troops or the communists come. "The soldiers may kill you if you don't tell them about the NPA," says one Mindanao farmer, "but the NPA will execute you as an informer if you do."

In their insurgency against the government, the communists combine urban activity with guerrilla fighting. They foment strikes, stir up teachers and students against the government, and infiltrate every respectable organization they can. Manila, Cebu, and Bacolod were to be the next targets when the "February revolution" took place, but Davao had been exposed to communist deviltry for years. In 1985 alone, the "sparrows" (communist death squads) killed thirty policemen among their hundreds of victims. In some of the city's poorer wards, the NPA was the only law there was. Citizens had to live by their wits, since "they were afraid of the left but could not trust the right."

THE MOUNTING THREAT

There is no doubt about the growth of the communist insurgency under Marcos, although the reasons for its growth and the exact figures may be open to question. When Marcos took office, the NPA admitted to no more than one hundred guerrillas. When martial law was declared, the NPA was still a ragged band of desperate men wandering among an indifferent populace with the army constantly at its heels. It did not move into Mindanao until 1976, when the AFP was dreadfully weakened by the Moro rebellion. Gradually it spread its operations from the mountains of northern Luzon through the Bicol Peninsula, through Samar, Negros, and Panay in the Visayas to the Christian-dominated territories in eastern and central Mindanao. From a sequence of anti-government encounters in isolated localities, it was transformed into a genuine nationwide movement, coordinated and directed by a sophisticated, dedicated leadership intent on achieving its long-term revolutionary goals.

By the end of the Marcos regime the NPA had grown into a force variously estimated at 15,000 to 22,500 guerrillas, with a supporting local militia of another 20,000 and a mass base of a million citizens. It operated in 62 of the country's 73 provinces and may have had control in as many as 20 percent of the 42,000 *barangays*. The annual death toll in murder, sabotage, and kidnapping incidents directly ascribable to the communist insurgency approached 5,000, equally divided among government troops, insurgents, and civilians. The carnage was worst in Mindanao.

These numbers are not absolute, but they are indicative. Figures about the strength of the NPA given out by the office of the president of the Philippines were varied to suit the immediate purpose of the press release: low, if the government wished to give the impression that the NPA was weak; high, if the objective was to emphasize the danger of incipient revolution. On the same day, President Marcos would give one set of numbers and his defense minister Enrile another. To attempt to tally figures reported by various regional commands with those reported by the central government, or to strike a balance between the conflicting claims of the government and the communists, was a hopeless task. Even American "official" figures were suspect; if they differed from Philippine figures, the intelligence community was not about to reveal its sources. Estimates of communist strength as given by the Pentagon to the U.S. Congress at budget time could conceivably have been tailored to suit the purposes of the administration.

COMMUNISM:
PHILIPPINE STYLE

To see why, or how, the communist insurgency expanded is not too difficult. Its strength was certainly not in its ideology. Anti-God communism is not popular in the Philippines, nor is any brand of quasi-socialism. Aside from a few radical intellectuals, no Filipino ever wanted a Soviet, Chinese, Vietnamese, or even a Nicaraguan-style revolution. Communism in the Philippines is short on ideology but long on opportunism. Furthermore, ideological indoctrination in the newly acquired cells began only *after* the NPA had established its control.

Nor was the communist growth to be explained by the unique qualities of its leadership. The Philippines produced no Mao Tsetung, Ho Chi Minh, or Joseph Stalin. The leaders from the university and in the field amply demonstrated their dedication and their toughness, but they were not supermen. Highly educated, they had no desire to fit into the existing social fabric. They have been described as "lawyers without clients, poets without readers, authors without an audience, cinematographers without opportunities, historians without classrooms, and journalists without employment." The leaders were fortunate in that the timing was ripe for any protest movement, and their followers were willing and able to endure the hardships to which they were exposed.

I would rule out the theory that the communists were the "good guys" in contrast to the "bad guys" on the other side. Testimony has been given in Mindanao that "They [the NPA] don't murder innocent people, they don't rape, pillage, and terrorize people the way the government soldiers do. They respect the church and private property, and most people here regard them as the only effective defense against official lawlessness." That was one view at a particular time in a specific locality, but similar testimonials have come from many other places. They must be appraised with care. The NPA tells all who will listen that it stands for social justice and human dignity. In various places, and when circumstances permit, the communists may look like Robin Hoods, but, when necessary, they shoot to kill.

The basic causes of communist success were the wretched performance of the Marcos government, the superior tactics of the guerrilla forces, and the abusive behavior of government troops. In failing to preserve law and order and to promote the general welfare, the government created the atmosphere of despair in which the communists flourished. Marcos glossed over the fundamental challenges he faced in the breakdown of political and social institutions at the local level. In the struggles between competing warlords, he settled for compromise. By dispensing favors, he bought compliance with his edicts. In spite of his profligacy, he was penurious in his treatment of the outlying provinces. His welfare plans brought neither food nor jobs for suffering people. His counter-insurgency operation was entrusted to armed forces that failed to do their job. The impotence of the government troops gave the communists all the freedom to maneuver they needed.

To the fighting forces, the insurgency was not one war, but many wars demanding a variety of tactics. The communists proved superior to the AFP in morale and adaptability. In the Cordillerra in northern Luzon, the communist leader, Father Balweg, though not a Tingguian, took up the cause of his neighbors who had lost their ricelands. "By birth," he said, "I am a Kalinga; in spirit, I am Tingguian." He symbolized the hope that the people of all tribes would stand together in the fight against the repressive government. Convinced that they were fighting in self-defense, he declared, "Even God gave a sword of fire to the good angels so they could fight the devil. We know the enemy, he does not know us. We can survive with leeches, snakes, chilly mountain nights, tall grass with razor sharp edges, malaria, and dysentery—he cannot." His intelligence network, his ability to "hit-and-run, hit-and-run, and drive the government crazy," and his mass support were models of organization and operation.

Outside of Luzon, the preferred tactic was to maneuver the government forces into spreading themselves thin and to strike where they were weakest. Catching patrols off guard was a daily occurrence. One raid on the Visayas Maritime Academy's armory netted the NPA more than 400 high-powered rifles. The government forces were as inept in their tactics as the guerrillas were clever. Aerial bombardments, free fire zones ("shoot anything that moves"), forcing thousands to flee their homes to strategic hamlets, and refusing to leave the main roads for convoys and troop movements made the army ineffective against the mobile NPA. For the army to keep its best regiments and best officers in Manila, leaving the fighting in the provinces to its least responsible and least capable units, was disastrous for the government.

Above all, it was the behavior of the military in the field that produced the greatest number of converts to the communist side. The good behavior of some troops, particularly the Marines and the Scout Rangers, has been thoroughly documented. But so has the brutality and the ruthlessness of some others, notably the Philippine Constabulary (PC) and the Civil Home Defense Forces (CHDF). Military and paramilitary personnel in the countryside were notorious for stealing rice and chickens, for forcing peasants to bring them food and beer, dig their foxholes, and supply them with women. At checkpoints on highways or rural roads slightly drunk personnel would extort money, pull off kidnappings, and torture—or even execute—suspected informers for the NPA.

Various old religious warrior sects, irregulars like the Ilagas and the Lost Command, and the CHDF gave the military its worst reputation. The sects and the irregulars were in it only for themselves. Although associated with the military, they would commit any crime for the sake of their own personal gain. The Lost Command—about 400 bandits in northern Mindanao—were notorious for extortion, robbery, rape, and killing. When they tired of robbing plantation owners, gold miners, fishermen, or coffee-bean growers, they would get jobs as security guards as a cover for their murder and thievery.

The 64,000 CHDF were the worst of the paramilitary offenders. Originally recruited by the simplest formula—"Sign up or be shot"— they were assigned as adjuncts to the AFP. Later they were transferred to the control of the town mayors or other civilian authorities, where, in effect, they became the private armies of the local warlords. For this arrangement, everybody was grateful to Marcos—except the people who suffered at the hands of the CHDF. As the symbol of authority and the guarantor of law and order, the CHDF was a total disaster. They were untrained, undisciplined, and unpaid—but armed—which was a sure-fire formula for corruption and abuse of their helpless victims. They were the primary source of all the stories of abduction, salvaging, and torture that gave the military its bad name. They were also the main reason why the government lost out in its battle against the communists for the hearts and minds of the people—for whom the choice was a matter of life and death.

By the time Marcos left the Philippines, he admitted that the communist insurgency had grown from an "irritant" into a threat to national existence. He was convinced that only he had the power, prestige, and wisdom to put it down. From his place of exile, he boasted that the Americans would have to call him back to handle it. Like it or not, *he* was the only alternative to the communists. He went so far as to say that it was possible allied troops would have to be called in to guarantee the nation's survival.

CHANGING STRATEGIES

Even before Marcos departed, some thoughtful leaders, including Defense Minister Enrile and some of his conscientious officers, were thinking of new policies for suppressing the communists. The most evident needs were the rebuilding of popular support for the government, boosting troop morale, and implementing new strategies for counter-insurgency. It was already clear that regaining the support of the masses would require more than bullets. Final victory over insurgency, according to Enrile, was not to be won by the armed forces alone. "We are the vanguards of the government's efforts to put together a program of economic and social development that will perhaps provide a secure base to contain the political impact of this problem on our people. The government must help the farmers and convince them it is their friend and not their oppressor."

With regard to military morale and new combat strategies, it was recognized by those who wished for better results that rewards for merit and punishment for wrongdoing must be implemented. The military must be converted into a people-oriented institution. Peace and order councils of civilians, the military, and representatives of the church should be created if the flow of communist victories in guerrilla combats was to be reversed. To have the concentration of military brains in Manila, and to have 50 percent of the total strength of the AFP in northern and eastern Mindanao, when 90 percent of the NPA's strength was elsewhere, was absolutely fatal.

In the last days of Marcos the common talk in Manila was that new strategies for dealing with the communists would be easy to implement if officers like Marine Colonel Rudy Biazon could only be found. A former slum kid from Pasay and Manila, his unit was sent to Davao when communist terrorism was at its height. Three or four people were being "liquidated" by the NPA or "salvaged" by the AFP every night—shot in cold blood in the lobbies of the best hotels, in offices, or in the streets. Col. Biazon did more than enforce the law. He made his men toe the line of honesty and protection for his people. He talked to detainees, returnees (ex-NPA men who surrendered), students, and any group he could assemble, about the menace of the communists and the frustrations of the constituted government. He visited homes and plantations and dared to enter into the *barangays* controlled by the NPA. Not surprisingly, the people of Davao petitioned to have him for their governor. By his own actions he pointed the way for Cory to follow in putting down the insurgency.

On the eve of President Aquino's assuming power, it was evident that the communists were having problems of their own: They suffered from the infirmities of overly rapid growth; they were in the midst of their own brand of rectification campaigns; and they were not sure how much Marxist ideology their leaders needed. With expansion, their organization came to depend more upon personalities than upon principles. As bright new recruits displaced the old guard, discipline became more difficult. Imprisonment weakened their leadership. Newcomers to the ranks lacked the vaunted qualities of the old revolutionaries. As the communist army grew, it needed more money, more arms, and different kinds of training. Because many of the cadres represented the only government in the areas in which they operated, the decentralization within the NPA threatened to degenerate into a kind of warlordism.

The party leadership was not prepared to come to grips with the Philippines after Marcos; they had overestimated Marcos's staying power and underestimated the strength of the People's Revolution. It was a serious mistake on their part not to join the opposition in the February elections. As long as Marcos was in Malacañang, the protest movements were popular. After Cory took over as president, the communists were not able to arrive at a consensus on questions that plagued them: What if Cory were genuine? What if her popularity should grow? What if her program should work? What if she should outshine the communists in the promise of a better life?

It was unsettling to think that the government—and not the communists—might be accepted as the champion of the masses; they could not think of operating without their mass base. The exercise of greater power in Metro Manila was a baffling prospect for them. They were not sure how to turn a negative protest psychology into a positive governing philosophy. It was one thing to strike a mill or to kill a manager; it was quite another to operate that mill for profit, or even for the well-being of the workers. To refuse to pay an unpopular tax was easy; to raise the money needed to balance a budget was infinitely more difficult. To circulate rumors against the administration was exciting; to think of themselves as the targets of the people's hatred was depressing. Manila was full of people who opposed the government, but no one among the higher-ups in the opposition was in favor of communism.

CORY AND
THE COMMUNISTS

Cory fully appreciates the seriousness of the communist insurgency. No one is better prepared than she to deal with the CPP, the NDF, and the NPA. Her experience with communism and the communists extends back to the Magsaysay days in central Luzon.

Basically, she argues that the insurgency stems not from Soviet or Chinese inspiration and support but from the sorry economic condition of the people, aggravated by Marcos, and the flaws in the political and social institutions against which they protest. She believes that near the end of the Marcos regime the military were on the right track in organizing the Peace and Order Councils to coordinate local security and national defense, but they did not go far enough—and they spoiled it all with their bad behavior.

As she sees it, there is a sharp distinction between the hard-core ideological communists and the mass base. For the hard-core, she would keep her powder dry and fight them with all the means at her disposal if they continue to resort to violence. To win the mass base to the fold of civilized society, she offers them food, medicine, hope for a new life, and a better alternative than the NPA. She accepts Mao Tse-tung's analysis that the people are the sea, and the guerrillas the fish that swim in it. Without the sea, the fish will die. Therefore, she would offer amnesty to all who forswear violence, and she would allow the CPP to operate as an ordinary political party.

As a candidate for the presidency, she explained her program in these words:

> I will use the power of the state to fight any force, whether communist or not, which will seek to overthrow our democratic government or destroy our cultural heritage, including our belief in God. But I will respect a communist's right, or anybody's right for that matter, peacefully to sell his ideas to others. I am confident that under a government that enjoys the confidence of the people, ideologies that run counter to our cultural and religious values will be rejected without need of bloodshed.

When she took over the presidency, she granted unconditional release to the communist leaders still held under detention. Included were Jose Marie Sison, the professor-theorist of the revolution, who had been held in solitary confinement for seven years, and Bernabe Buscayno—also known as Commander Dante—who had converted the ragged band of outlaws into the most formidable communist resistance force in the world today. As she proceeded with her military reforms and worked on plans for rehabilitation of the insurgents, she sought the help of the church in raising money to support pilot programs for the surrendering "returnees." Her immediate objective was to persuade the NPA that the government was not against their ideals, only their methods. "I am not asking the communists to give up their stern vision of a just society," she said. "I am only asking them to give our people a chance to work out their own version of a just and progressive society in peace." She appealed to all: "Let us give peace a chance."

She believed the time was ripe to talk with communist leaders about a cease-fire and a possible amnesty. They, too, were sick of the fighting. They were temporarily embarrassed by their gross miscalculation in remaining aloof from the events that had forced Marcos out of office. They had lost the opportunity to lead a people's revolution, and, worse, they had lost their identity with the people's cause.

As her representatives to negotiate with the communists at the national level, she appointed Jose Diokno (later replaced by Teofisto Guingona) and Ramon Mitra. The communists appointed Satur Ocampo (the business editor of the *Manila Times* in pre-Marcos days, who had spent nine years in detention before his escape in May 1985) and Antonio Zumel (a member of the politburo of the CPP and the head of the NDF). Their meetings were to be in secret and their agenda kept under wraps. It was assumed that they would start their discussions with basics—the logistics and terms of getting the Red Fighters out of the hills—and go on to fundamental, long-range policy differences between the government and the CPP.

That the negotiations were slow in achieving results was not surprising. No one expected a mass surrender of the NPA or a dramatic slowdown in the scale of fighting. Each side recognized that the other was retraining and regrouping as negotiations continued. The new communist leadership—Rodolfo Salas (arrested by the military in the fall of 1986), Rafael Baylosis, and Antonio Zumel, all confirmed ideologues—did not trust Cory any more than they had trusted Marcos. She, too, was a capitalist, dominated by the Americans (according to them), and the feudal system was still intact.

Antonio Zumel stated his position candidly: "We will continue to conduct tactical offensives, targeting especially military units that are known to be abusive, provincial warlords once protected by the Marcos regime, and certain paramilitary units said to have a long record of human rights violations." He said that it was daydreaming to think the communists would ever surrender or give up the armed struggle as long as the basic conditions for carrying arms were still there. "On the other hand," he said, "if military reforms are instituted, attacks against the NPA halted, serious land reform undertaken, a tough stand taken against foreign intervention in terms of both the military bases and economic matters, a cease-fire is possible."

While negotiations were being conducted in Manila, simultaneous discussions in the major battle zones were being held independently between local military commanders and representatives of the NPA. In some places, local officials, businessmen, and the clergy participated. The discussants in each region were seeking a formula to reduce or end hostilities in their own particular locality.

It is difficult to capsulize what was actually happening in the fight against the insurgents during the ten months of fighting and talking because reports from the field were fragmentary and unreliable. For example, on June 1, 1986, the deputy chief of staff for operations reported that since the present government came to power, 47 incidents of surrender—involving 1,484 rebels, of whom 103 were regular fighters, 320 part-time guerrillas, and 1,061 sympathizers who form the insurgents' mass base—had occurred. Such precision is re-

Negotiating with the NPA: President Aquino meeting with guerrilla leader Father Conrado Balweg in the Cordillera in northern Luzon.

markable from an intelligence apparatus that rates a C-minus at best. In the first six months of the Aquino administration, the number of guerrillas was supposed to have grown by one-third, to a total of 22,500. Average contacts (any fight between a soldier and a suspected communist is called a contact) in 1986 were down a bit from 1985, but still averaged 9 a day, with 11 deaths—4 soldiers, 4 rebels, and 3 civilians. All that can be said for certain is that the fighting continued while negotiations were under way.

Eyewitness accounts from northern Luzon affirmed the continued occurrence of skirmishes and ambushes. Father Balweg, who was more interested in minority rights for his fellow tribesmen than in straight communist ideology, and some of his companions split from the CPP/NPA to form a Cordillera Peoples Liberation Army. Nuns in Samar went right into communist territory to plead the government's case. The largest of the eighteen regions into which the CPP divided the Philippines, Samar was the site of one of the main NPA training centers.

In Cagayan de Oro, according to Arthur Zich, writing in the *National Geographic* in July 1986, "There is a different feeling in the land." In *barangay* Claveria, some 1,000 people—men, women, and children—whom the NPA had considered part of their mass base had gone over to the government side after the election. In reprisal, the NPA rounded them up, together with their cows, chickens, pigs, and carabaos, and were in the process of herding them toward a labor farm when elements of a government Scout Ranger battalion rumbled up and rescued them, virtually without firing a shot. Then the Rangers choppered in with food and medicine to help the people. Said the mayor, "We estimate that since the election, the NPA has lost 50 hard-core rebels. The people are sick of killing, and Cory offers us a fresh start." Thus, in three of the worst communist-infested areas of the Philippines, the policy of reconciliation—with the help of the church—made its impact, if ever so slight, on the status and program of the NPA.

In Davao, Cory worked hardest to implement her own program, aided and abetted by a locally appointed presidential commission on reconciliation and by a staunch new regional commander, Brigadier General Jose Magno. She was advised that any program in Davao, to be successful for the returnees, must provide that the government buy (not sequester) rebel arms, give each returnee cash, a piece of land, some farm implements, seed, and a loan to help him with his first harvest. Chito Ayala, a highly respected plantation owner in the area, estimated that such a program would cost $1,000 per man, which is far less than the cost of maintaining an army.

In May 1986, Cory traveled to Davao—in a van with tinted, bullet-proof windows—where she met with a group of 168 rebel returnees to discuss with them her plan for a cease-fire and amnesty. She told the rebels she recognized their obvious bravery and their acute sense of justice. She insisted, however, that any truce would have to protect the honor of the military. If a truce were to be agreed upon and then violated, "This would be a signal of the failure of negotiations and the resumption of hostilities." The rebels asked her for assurances of safety and assistance to lead a new life. She replied that while negotiations continued, she would hold General Magno responsible for their safety. But, she cautioned them, "If I were to promise you that I will give you jobs, then you know that I will not be telling you the truth."

When President Aquino visited Washington, President Reagan reportedly indicated that he was displeased with the way she was handling the communists. Her calm reply was, "That is too bad, but it is I who will decide just what we do in our country." Knowing that she could not hope to induce many communists to give up their armed struggle, she was nevertheless determined to continue her peaceful efforts to bring the insurgency to an end. Hard-liners on both sides were totally opposed to the negotiations between the government and the communists. On the government side, the military were displeased. Convinced that the communists were committed to a godless, bloodthirsty insurgency, out to destroy democracy and seize absolute power, they accused Cory of becoming soft on communism, surrounded as she was by the leftists in her government. She was wrong, they maintained, if she thought that any agreement with the communists was worth the paper it was written on. Furthermore, the national representatives of the CPP had no way of enforcing their decisions on the diverse local communist situations.

Hard-liners on the communist side were just as uncompromising. The military, they maintained, acquiesced in negotiations only to allow themselves breathing space. They argued that Cory would never make meaningful concessions to their long-term demands but would only offer harmless compromises on minor matters while she built up her armed forces. The hard-core communists proclaimed, "We will fight until imperialism, feudalism, and bureaucratic capitalism

During the cease-fire, the soldiers of the New People's Army in Bataan emerge from their mountain hideouts in response to a guarantee of safety.

are eliminated from our country. We don't care who the enemy is, Americans or Filipinos, we will fight and keep on fighting. We are the Philippine people." They regarded the offer of legalization of the CPP as nothing more than a clever capitalist ploy.

Negotiations for a cease-fire degenerated into a war of words exacerbated by the media. The communists gained a great deal of public sympathy with their appeal for "land, not bombs; bread, not bullets; milk, not armalites [machine guns]; and life, not death." Cory realized that while negotiations dragged on, the communists were scoring points in the propaganda war.

On November 27, the two sides announced in Manila that they had agreed on a cease-fire to last sixty days, beginning December 10. Alleged infractions of the agreement would be monitored by local and national committees, while the negotiators would continue their discussions of long-range substantive issues. This arrangement would permit the government to concentrate on the campaign for the constitution without fear of renewed hostilities and would make it possible for the soldiers of the NPA to visit their families and friends

The New People's Army in Mindanao during the cease-fire urged a "no" vote on the new Constitution.

without risking capture or arrest. For the first time in eighteen years Christmas in the Philippines promised to be a season of peace.

During the sixty days of truce, the armed forces remained on alert and stepped up their training. So did the communists. In Manila, the communists held press conferences, made speeches, and put up posters advertising the positive aspects of their program. In Samal, Bataan, they put on a media event. Especially for the benefit of foreign correspondents, some 800 townspeople, complete with red banners and a brass band, welcomed fifty rifle-toting soldiers of the NPA down from the hills and showered them with cigarettes and Christmas gifts. Communists everywhere took the fullest advantage of the lull in the fighting.

RENEWED
VIOLENCE

When the Manila truce expired on February 8, 1987, the insurgency situation throughout the Philippines returned to the *status quo ante*. Announcing that the truce was over, Cory urged her officers to hit hard and to retaliate against any NPA attack. General Ramos explained that although this was a declaration of all-out war against the rebels, there would still be negotiations. For their part, the Communists declared that she had capitulated to the militarists, with the full support of the United States. Therefore, "We will hit all enemy units, be it regular, paramilitary, or private armies conducting counterinsurgency operations or harassing and intimidating the civilian population." In the first week of renewed hostilities, the government reported seventeen insurgency-related incidents in which thirty-eight persons were killed, of whom twenty-two were rebels, eleven soldiers, four police officers, and one a civilian. There was no significant difference in casualty rates before and after the cease-fire.

In countering the insurgency, the government's task is not so much to reach another flimsy agreement with the communist central command as to win the battles against the insurgents in the many isolated localities throughout the Philippines. The politburo of the CPP may write the party program and do the central planning, but it is still the scattered self-reliant communist groups that adapt those programs and plans to their own local circumstances. They fight for their survival, or welfare, in their own way with very little help from the party center. This may change, of course, but at this stage the government is dealing far more with disorganized violence than with a unified national communist revolutionary movement. Ultimate victory will depend upon much more than military superiority.

Nothing handicaps President Aquino more than the sorry state of the Philippine military. Upon the expiration of the cease-fire, General Ileto himself stated publicly, "Our soldiers' morale is so low it will take a generation to reform the military, unite everybody and weed out the bad ones." Low morale makes the military a very weak reed to lean upon. Cory may make a brave show of declaring all-out war on dissidents of the right or left, but she is not ready to abandon her policy of reconciliation. She still feels the insurgency will never end unless the millions of very poor in the Philippines become convinced that they can find a better way of life in cooperating with the government than in pursuing their communist ideology.

8

"Many Filipinos feel
as I do. We want
you to get the hell out of there."

Ambassador S.P. Lopez in an academic
conference at Stanford, August 1983

FOREIGN RELATIONS: BEFORE AQUINO

Cory and most of her colleagues grew up at a time when foreign affairs and U.S.-Philippine relations were practically synonymous, when the survival and welfare of the Philippines depended on the patronage and goodwill of the United States. But this is transition time. The baton is being passed to Cory's children and their generation. The Philippines, not the United States, is the heart of their existence. To them, the outside world is not only the United States, but all nations. The more the Filipinos become involved in the complexities of the modern world, the more their nationalism is bound to grow.

The attitudes and actions of the Aquino administration must be judged and measured in the light of its place in Philippine history. The captive of its own past, it must honor the precedents that it has inherited, and, within the limitations upon its freedom of action, make the most of its opportunities. It cannot escape the consequences of colonialism or ignore the good and the bad in the American heritage. Even World War II and the granting of independence (more precisely, the relinquishing of American sovereignty) have left their share of painful memories. Independence brought its own benefits and also its responsibilities. In conducting its own diplomacy, the Philippines had to learn how to stand up for itself. Emotions had to be curbed and demands kept within reason.

A preview of the foreign relations program of the Aquino administration begins with an analysis of the roots of the policies that it inherited, examines the alleged limitations on Philippine sovereignty imposed as conditions of independence, notes the rise of Philippine nationalism, and calls attention to the expansion of the nation's diplomatic horizons beyond the United States.

THE COLONIAL
HERITAGE

Irked by their status as Indios, or second-class citizens, Filipinos began their struggle for independence—that is, for respectability, freedom, and even democracy—against the Spanish. (Ninoy Aquino's grandfather was a general associated with Aguinaldo in that fight.) When the Americans displaced the Spanish in 1898, the struggle continued. Filipinos fought as bravely and with as high a proportion of losses and casualties as the Vietnamese suffered in fighting the French at a later date. The Filipinos lost their fight, but not their strong desire for independence.

The Americans took the Philippines as a prize of war and administered it as an ordinary colony. In two years of fighting against Filipino guerrillas, atrocities were frequent, and in the following two years of military rule, the Americans paid little attention to the sensibilities of the Filipinos. When a civil government was established, its mission was to govern for the happiness, peace, and prosperity of the people of the Philippine Islands, and to repect their customs, habits, and even their prejudices. As a colony of the United States, the Philippines was incorporated into the American international trading system and given the protection of the American fleet.

The record shows the ambivalence of the United States toward the Philippines: selfish in its efforts to preserve the colonial character of the Philippine economy and thus perpetuate the economic dependence of the Filipinos on American capital, and in its wish to transform the Philippines into a permanent auxiliary base for the United States in the Pacific; enlightened in bringing to the Philippines the rule of law, self-government, a system of public education, better roads and harbor facilities, pure drinking water, and improved standards of public health.

Unwilling to subject their own national interests to the whims of the oligarchs who rose to prominence in the Philippine government, the Americans did not allow the Filipinos to take the initiative in developing their own infant industries or in preparing themselves for economic independence. Americans were blamed for clamping on the Filipinos a "colonial mentality," implying political inferiority, economic vassalage, intellectual incompetence, and cultural corruption.

In the opinion of many Filipinos, the most devastating effects of colonialism have been psychological. The hot pursuit of things American has warped traditional values and diminished the Filipinos' pride in themselves. Anybody who made extra money in the colonial period wanted to spend it for American cars, American-style homes, or a trip to the United States. Filipino deference to Americans came dangerously close to servility. Filipinos bought American books and magazines, flocked to Hollywood movies, wore American-style clothes, and adopted American music and basketball as their own. Because more Filipinos spoke English than any one of their native dialects, English became the *lingua franca* throughout the islands.

Reactions varied from individual to individual, and from family to family. Some Filipinos were frustrated, many were jealous. Old-line families, like the Aquinos, accepted American things and values, which they believed to be intrinsically good and desirable, but they were dedicated to preserving the Filipino way of life. Most of all they wanted an independent nation, completely free from the United States. For Filipinos—Asian in geography and ancestry—to be tied to the apron strings of an overseas power was unnatural and untenable. Whatever else any Philippine administration wished to accomplish, it would first rid itself of the last vestiges of colonialism.

Nothing infuriates a Filipino more than to suggest he has a colonial mind. A recent outburst by my good friend S.P. Lopez at an academic conference illustrates the depth and intensity of Filipino emotions tied up in colonialism. He said (in referring to the military bases):

> You know the trouble with colonialism? It is so much better to talk about it with the colonist rather than [with] the colonized. It is nicer, so much more pleasant. You can stand at the top of the stairs and talk to us below. But the fellow down below is something else. We Filipinos have been there for 450 years. I hope that gives you an idea of why I feel as

I do. And why many Filipinos feel as I do. We want you to get the hell out of there!

WORLD
WAR II

When the end of colonialism came into sight with the establish-ment of the Commonwealth government in 1935, it seemed that the era of hard feelings would give way as the Philippines recovered its full sovereignty. Such was not to be the case. World War II in some respects drew Filipinos and Americans closer together; in other re-spects, it drove them further apart. Filipinos and Americans who fought together at Bataan and Corregidor, and again in Leyte and in Luzon, felt the closest comradeship during combat. Japan's war was not against the Filipinos; it was against the Americans in the Philip-pines. But during the bombing and the exchange of artillery fire, it was primarily Philippine property that was destroyed and Filipino lives that were lost. The government of the Philippines did not receive the amount of compensation it believed it deserved. Nor did Filipino veterans of the U.S. armed forces get back pay and other benefits equal to those later granted to American veterans, although they had stood side by side with Americans in facing the dangers of battle. They felt that they were treated unjustly. They felt, and still feel, that they were victims of discrimination.

With the return of MacArthur and the American liberation forces, it was difficult to find many people who had much sympathy for those Filipinos who had accepted official responsibilities under the Japanese. The popular belief, particularly among Americans, was that the ex-commonwealth officials who had not been able to leave with Quezon were bound by their oaths of office to remain unswervingly loyal to the United States. Many in Washington argued that the Fili-pinos who were left behind were like Quislings in Europe and should be punished. But they were not like Quislings. Up to the very time the Japanese entered the city of Manila, the Filipinos who were left behind cooperated fully and freely with the Americans.

On January 2, 1942, at 3:00 A.M.—a mere four hours before the Japanese troops entered Manila en force—as the senior American of the High Commissioner's staff left in Manila, I telephoned Jorge Var-gas, my counterpart in the Philippine government, to ask if there was anything more that either of us could do to meet the imminent oc-cupation. His answer was "no," but his devotion to our cause was abundantly clear. He and his colleagues were left entirely on their own, without any protection or prospect of help from the Americans. Whatever arrangements they made with the Japanese subsequently had to be as the result of *force majeure*, with nothing less than their own survival at stake.

With the election of Aquino and Laurel, both of whose families played a prominent role during the Japanese occupation, discussion of the role of the collaborators has taken on a new interest. For a long time the collaborators were treated with disdain, while well-known guerrilla leaders were hailed as heroes. Then the pendulum gradually swung in the reverse direction. The case of Senator Aquino, Ninoy's father, is typical. A distinguished official in the Quezon government, he decided he could expedite independence for the Philippines by accepting an office under the Japanese. His attitude was, "I don't care who gives us independence as long as we start independence by ourselves." The Japanese made him responsible for running the *Kalibapi*, the Association for Service to the New Philippines, that was supposed to unite the entire adult population into a single supraparty.

When the news of his action reached the United States by short-wave, Americans were appalled. But he did his job well. When the Americans returned to liberate the Philippines, they would have arrested the leading collaborators, but the Japanese had flown them to Japan. There they were safe until the Americans occupied Japan. Then the Americans arrested Aquino, Laurel, Vargas, and others who gave themselves up voluntarily to the occupation authorities. They were kept in Sugamo prison for nearly a year while MacArthur was carrying out his reconciliation policy with Japan. By the time they were freed and returned to Manila, Senator Aquino's health had been seriously impaired. Suffering a series of heart attacks, he died in Manila in December 1947. The new Philippine attitude toward the ex-collaborators was expressed in Senator Recto's funeral oration, delivered at Aquino's bier:

> You were worthless to them in this game of power politics where they have always wanted to use Filipinos as lackeys, field hands, and cannon fodder. That is why Hirohito continues on the throne of his glorious ancestors while you were thrown into a prison cell, where you got the disease that would take you to the grave.

Rest in peace, faithful servant of your people! When minds have recovered their serenity and intellects their discernment, when your countrymen have learned to work, live, and think only for one nation and one flag, without a lackey's servility or a courtier's fawning before any foreign power, then they will remember your splendid achievements and the noble example of your nationalism, virile and blameless, and they will call you a true patriot because you were always a true Filipino.

How could anyone be condemned as a traitor to his country and his people who had displayed the courage of Claro Recto? On assuming the portfolio of foreign affairs *under the Japanese*, he dared to declare that "We Filipinos owe no allegiance to any foreign power; the government of this republic is a government by Filipinos for Filipinos alone; the constitution we have sworn to defend is our constitution; the president, whose courage, wisdom, statesmanship, and patriotism constitute the strongest bulwark of our freedom during this period of trial, is our own president." No wonder the People's Court, under Lorenzo Tanada, exonerated Recto. In the judgment of the court, Recto "not only did not make common cause with the enemy, but, on the contrary, continued at all times to be faithful and loyal to his country and the allied cause."

Dr. Jose Laurel, Doy's father, who had accepted office as president of the Philippines under the Japanese, was nominated for president on the Nacionalista ticket to oppose the incumbent Quirino in 1949. Laurel was defeated in an election that was notoriously crooked, even by Filipino standards. Until the day of his death, he continued to serve his government. He is best known for the Laurel-Langley Agreement, which regulated U.S.-Philippine trade for twenty years until the expiration of the agreement in 1974.

Americans often observe that Filipino nationalism and its counterpart—anti-Americanism—are growing stronger as the common experience of the colonial relationship and World War II fade into the background. That is only part of the story. Nationalism was always strong. Some who lived through the last days of the colonial period and World War II have golden memories; others look back on those times with sadness and pain. Philippine historians increasingly overlook the former and emphasize the latter. Memory only accentuates the burgeoning spirit of nationalism that affects the decisions of any Filipino dealing with foreign affairs.

THE DARK SIDE
OF INDEPENDENCE

To most Filipinos, the achievement of independence was a dream come true, a promise of freedom, happiness, and greater prosperity. At the time, no one looked on the dark side. Coming of age meant responsibility for doing for themselves the things that had formerly been done for them. The Americans could no longer be counted on to look after Filipino interests. Whatever the Americans would do in the Philippines would be for the protection and promotion of American interests. Filipinos would benefit from the American connection only as their interests coincided. Acting in accordance with the new order was difficult for both Americans and Filipinos; the Americans were accustomed to assuming special rights and privileges in the Philippines, and the Filipinos found it hard to break the habit of special dependence on the United States. As the two nations drifted apart in their world outlook, their differences multiplied. Because the good feelings between them had been so genuine and long-enduring, their mutual grievances were difficult to resolve.

The parting of the ways was signaled in the interim between the Japanese surrender (August 15, 1945) and the American proclamation of Philippine independence (July 4, 1946). Shortly after the Americans returned to the Philippines, the U.S. Congress passed the Tydings Rehabilitation Act and the Bell Trade Act. The former appropriated money to compensate for losses sustained in the Philippines *provided* the new Philippine government would accept the latter act, which defined conditions for American trade and investment in the Philippines. In the American view, the Tydings Act was magnanimous, generous, and unprecedented. The Bell Act was a reasonable price to ask to entice American business back to the Philippines.

The Filipinos saw it otherwise. To the Filipinos, the Tydings Act was far too little and far too slow in implementation. The Bell Act—particularly in the "parity" clause giving Americans and Filipinos parity of rights in developing natural resources and operating public utilities in the Philippines—was a nefarious scheme to perpetuate American control over the wealth of the Philippines. To force the Filipinos to amend their constitution in order to receive the benefits of the Tydings Act looked to them like a heartless, immoral, and arrogant display of American power.

On July 4, 1946, the Americans and the Filipinos signed the Treaty of General Relations, legally putting the relationships between the two nation-states on a basis of recognized equality. To the Americans, this was the promise redeemed. But the Filipinos demurred. They called attention to Article I:

> The United States of America agrees to withdraw and surrender ... all rights of possession, supervision, jurisdiction, control of sovereignty existing and exercised by the United States of America in and over the territory and the people of the Philippine Islands, *except* the use of such bases, necessary appurtenances to such bases, and the rights incident thereto, as the United States of America, by agreement with the Republic of the Philippines, may deem necessary to retain for the mutual protection of the Republic of the Philippines and of the United States of America.

In the eyes of the Filipinos, this article is a flaw in the grant of independence and an infringement of Philippine sovereignty. Sanctioned by treaty, it cannot be removed except by treaty. It is Exhibit No. 1 in the campaign to revise the entire treaty relationship between the two countries.

In March 1947, the Philippines (still under President Roxas) signed the first Military Bases Agreement (MBA) and the first Military Assistance Agreement (MAA) with the United States. At the time, these agreements were willingly accepted by the Filipinos as guarantees of *mutual* security. Later generations have blistered these agreements as clear violations of Philippine sovereignty and evidences of a subtle brand of American neo-imperialism.

The original MBA provided that certain lands for base use should be granted to the United States "free of rent." In sixteen bases (including Subic Bay and Clark Field), the United States was given rights to control the base areas; to improve and deepen harbors; to construct access roads, tracks, and pipelines; and to install associated facilities for navigational and electronic purposes. Further rights granted to Americans included the right to use land and coastal areas for periodic maneuvers, for additional staging areas, for bombing and gunnery ranges, and for immediate airfields. American personnel serving on the bases were given extraterritorial status and exemption from Philippine internal revenue taxes, and were allowed to operate their own postal service. The MBA was to remain in force for ninety-nine years.

The MAA provided that military aid was to be given the Philippines for development of the armed forces in the form of arms, ammunition, equipment, and supplies; certain army and naval assets; and training by the Americans. The agreement also defined the kind of military assistance available to the Philippines both in terms of advice and actual armament. Under this agreement, a Joint U.S. Military Advisory Group (JUSMAG) was set up in the Philippines as part of the U.S. diplomatic mission; selected students of the Armed Forces of the Philippines were sent to schools and military installations in the United States for advanced training; and arrangements were made for the exchange of classified military equipment and information. Article XX of the agreement states that any purchase of military hardware to be made by the Philippines shall be made only on the basis of mutual agreement between the two governments. The MAA was to be valid for five years and subject to renewal.

President Roxas (1946-1948) pursued a single-minded diplomatic course: to follow "in the glistening wake of America, whose sure advance with mighty prow breaks for smaller craft the waves of fear." During the administrations of his successors, Quirino (1948-1953) and Magsaysay (1953-1957), the balance of power in the world shifted dramatically with the rise of the communist nations. The United States, in the Korean War and in the global confrontation with the Soviet Union, was forced to divide its energies and resources into smaller portions, leaving less for the Philippines.

"SPECIAL RELATIONS"

Meanwhile, the Republic of the Philippines found the way of independence to be much rockier than it had anticipated. It continued to seek "special relations" with the United States, but it received less help than it wanted or needed. In 1950 the Quirino administration received from the United States an agreement to make available $250 million over a period of five years for economic aid.

Following the Korean War, the Philippines signed, in 1951, the Treaty of Peace with Japan and the Mutual Defense Treaty with the United States. The Mutual Defense Treaty provides that in the event of an attack on the Philippines, the United States will act in accordance with its constitutional processes. Senator Recto, the patron saint of the Philippine nationalists, led the opposition to the treaty. He argued that the American commitment was vague and amounted to no commitment at all. He wanted the Philippines to have the benefit of the NATO formula, stipulating that an armed attack against either of the contracting parties in the Pacific area should be considered an attack against both. In the event of such an armed attack against the Philippines, the United States would assist the Philippines by taking immediate action to repel the attack and to restore and maintain the security of the Philippines and of the Pacific area. Note Recto's bitter words on the floor of the Senate:

> In the world parliament of the United Nations, it is no more difficult to predict that the Philippines will vote with the American Union than that the Ukraine will vote with the Soviet Union.... We have a mendicant foreign policy, and as beggars we cannot be choosers. We can safely be ignored, taken for granted, dictated to, made to wait at the door, hat in hand, to go in only when invited.... Dependent entirely on American arms, we find it increasingly difficult to procure them. Having rested our hopes on American bases, we find them unmanned, dismantled, and in the great majority abandoned, so that rather than sources of protection they may become targets for attack.

In later years the argument would change. It was not that the bases were unmanned, dismantled, or abandoned, but that they were overmanned and overly equipped, particularly with nuclear weapons. But the Recto mystique prevailed, and its fundamental premise was that "rather than sources of protection, the bases have become targets for attack."

President Magsaysay, after the defeat of the French at Dienbienphu and the Geneva Convention, which ended the French-Vietnamese hostilities, brought the Philippines closely into line with U.S. policies. He authorized the negotiation of the Laurel-Langley trade agreement, which became effective in 1956, and which put an end to the most galling features of the existing trade patterns by prescribing conditions for special economic relations that would last until July 4, 1974. In this agreement, some privileges were granted the Philippines but the nation was far from satisfied. Disappointed at not receiving even more favorable terms for its sugar and cigars in the American market, the Philippines complained of shabby treatment by its powerful trading partner. One Philippine congressman went so far as to say that, as a result of American shortsightedness, the prevailing attitude toward the United States in the Philippines might well change from admiration and hero-worship to disillusionment and hostility.

Entirely in sympathy with the U.S. government's perception of the menace of international communism, President Magsaysay signed the Southeast Asia Treaty of Collective Defense, commonly called the Manila Pact. Eight nations (the United States, the United Kingdom, France, Australia, New Zealand, Pakistan, Thailand, and the Philippines) agreed that in the event of aggression by means of armed attack in the treaty area against any of the parties, the signatories would act to meet the common danger in accordance with their constitutional processes. They would consult together to agree on measures of common defense if any one of them considered the inviolability, territorial integrity, sovereignty, or political independence of any party to the treaty threatened other than by armed attack. Critical Filipinos argued that this treaty was not really for the regional defense of Southeast Asia; it was a cover for "U.S. aggression and proneness to interfere in the internal affairs of the smaller nations of Asia, including the Philippines."

During the Magsaysay administration, strong evidence of an intense national spirit began to appear. Magsaysay opposed the fanatic economic nationalist movement as an attempt to "cut our own people off from the outside world by a wall of suspicion, distrust, and hatred." The issue of ultra-nationalism, which was readily equated with anti-Americanism, divided the followers of Magsaysay (including Carlos Romulo) from the disciples of Senator Recto.

Magsaysay himself, as intensely patriotic as any of his colleagues, never minded being referred to as pro-American. He saw no conflict between being pro-Filipino and pro-American. When Recto decided to oppose President Magsaysay, who planned to run for reelection in 1957, Magsaysay declared to one of his friends, "Let Recto run for the presidency on an anti-American platform. I will run as a pro-American and beat him."

While the government remained friendly to the United States, political orators, together with teachers and students in the universities, columnists and commentators, ambitious native businessmen, and left-wing agitators, fanned the flames of Philippine chauvinism—and anti-Americanism. History was reinterpreted to blame the colonial heritage for all the ills of the Philippines. According to the revisionists, the Americans during their tenure had been insensitive to the feelings of Asians, and this had made the subject Filipinos dishonest and evasive. The new nationalists called for the aggressive assertion of their Filipino identity.

THE RISE
OF NATIONALISM

Arguments over the Bases. The administrations of Presidents Garcia (1957-1961) and Macapagal (1961-1965) witnessed the high tide of Filipino nationalism. Although it subsided during the Marcos era, it can be expected to rise again when the Aquino government gets around to the sticky problems of foreign relations. When, for example, the military bases come up for review, it is inevitable that emotions will flare on both sides. Filipinos will make the same demands they have made for four decades, but now will be tougher negotiators because of the confidence they have gained by the People's Revolution.

In the last days of Magsaysay (1955-1957), Senator Recto missed no opportunity to lambast the president for his slavish, pro-American attitude. Recto's chief complaint was against the Mutual Defense Treaty. He argued that for Philippine security under the Americans, a new treaty with an automatic retaliation clause was essential. The American commitment must be that "any armed attack against the Philippines would involve an attack against the U.S. forces stationed there and against the United States, and would instantly be repelled." Philippine nationalists almost unanimously shared Recto's opinion.

The speaker of the Philippine House of Representatives, Jose P. Laurel, Jr. (Doy's older brother), in 1956 spoke out against the United States with unusual bluntness. He said:

> It is claimed in platitudes, now tired and empty, that as the prodigious child of American enlightenment we are the living example in Asia of democracy in action. Nonsense. We are under the heel of a new oppression that shatters not our bodies but our illusions, and subjects us to a great disenchantment because it takes the form of discrimination, prejudice, and ingratitude, and comes with a profession of friendship.

A succession of incidents at some of the military bases at the end of the 1950s involving rape, assault, destruction of property, and even the "shooting of Filipinos like dogs" inflamed public opinion and triggered a series of negotiations aimed at curing some of the alleged evils of the bases. The Filipinos sought new understandings on matters of sovereignty, delimitation of base areas, operational rights of Americans and Filipinos, a time limit on American usage of the bases, and respective powers of jurisdiction.

In subsequent agreements negotiated in 1953 and again in 1966, the United States acceded to some of the Philippine demands. The United States unequivocally acknowledged the sovereignty of the Philippines over all bases in its territory. Unused bases and extra lands were returned to the Philippines. The Philippines demanded and received the right to be consulted if the bases were to be used for military and combat purposes "other than those conducted in accordance with treaties to which the Philippines is a party." The Philippines was also given the right to be consulted on the use of the bases in the event of war or as launching sites for long-range nuclear missiles. The period of American occupation of the bases was reduced in 1966 from the original ninety-nine years as agreed upon in 1947 to twenty-five years, ending in 1991. To find answers to the problems of jurisdiction over American servicemen accused of committing crimes off base and off duty proved impossible.

During these negotiations, it was clear that Philippine questions about the bases were neither prompted by innate anti-Americanism nor communist inspired. They rather reflected a hardheaded Philippine concern for its own national interests. The use of American facilities on the Philippine bases was designed for the *mutual* security of the two nations, not for the United States alone. Filipinos wanted to make sure they were not shortchanged.

The argument over the bases has consistently revolved around personal attitudes. Filipinos hated the superior airs of the Americans. They resented being wholly dependent on American strength and knowing that their destiny was jeopardized with every cast of the American diplomatic dice. They disliked the honkytonks and the sin-cities surrounding the bases. It was galling to contrast the shabby poverty-stricken Philippine countryside with the American oases of luxury, where "a single shelf in the PX would feed a whole *barrio* for a year and where the famed American way of life appears to Filipinos like a Babylonian dream."

An anti-U.S., anti-Marcos protest in downtown Manila. There were far fewer Filipinos here than were lined up across the street seeking visas to enter the United States.

Filipino First. In addition to the problems of the bases, economic issues—trade and investments, U.S. "aid," and Philippine claims— swelled the tide of Philippine nationalism. In keeping with the slogan of "Filipino First," the National Economic Council, under the chairmanship of former Senator Dr. Jose Locsin, passed a resolution in 1958 encouraging Filipinos to engage in vital enterprises and industries so as to increase their share of total economic activity. A series of laws and regulations expanded the area of government ownership and planning and gave Filipinos a more significant role in economic development. The climate for foreign investment became more oppressive. At the same time, whether because of Philippine legislation or the general improvement in world economic conditions, Philippine income and production figures showed a marked improvement. Financial reserves strengthened, and under the Laurel-Langley Agreement, the international trade balance turned favorable. Filipinos began to invest in new enterprises and to buy out many of the long-established American firms.

Filipinos sought to displace the entrenched American position in import and export services, the travel industry, mining, utilities, petroleum products, life insurance, real estate, and every phase of industrial expansion. They endeavored to curb the activities of those foreigners, chiefly Americans, whom they considered foreign exploiters, profiteers, adventurers, and ordinary carpetbaggers. They resented the very word "aid," alleging that "aid" programs were primarily designed to promote American interests and only incidentally to contribute to the welfare of Filipinos. They believed their sacrifices in World War II entitled them to more "aid" than the Americans could ever give them. Political and commercial circles in the Philippines were infuriated when the U.S. Congress refused to honor the $800 million in claims for losses due to gold devaluation, unpaid war damages, processing taxes collected by the United States on sugar and coconut oil, and back pay for Philippine veterans. Nationalists argued, "If the United States paid us what they owe us, there would be no need for aid."

While nationalism and anti-foreignism flourished, President Garcia (1957-1961) labored to keep official U.S.-Philippine relations on a friendly basis. In an address to the U.S. Congress in 1959, he renewed his vow "to stand by the United States as long as her leadership of the Free World continues to be so nobly dedicated to the supreme cause of world freedom and peace." In entertaining President Eisenhower in Manila, he assured his guest that the upsurge of nationalism could not weaken or dissolve the ties of friendship that had bound the United States and the Philippines so closely together for fifty years. As a matter of fact, anti-Americanism was on the decline and goodwill on the rise when President Macapagal moved into Malacañang.

Once in power, the Liberals, under President Macapagal (1961-1965), launched a successful campaign against the excesses of nationalism. The Liberals called the Nacionalistas "patrioteers," or racketeers of patriotism, vilifying foreign firms while scrambling to get jobs as legal retainers and living like rajahs while the masses lived in want. Anchoring his foreign policy in good relations with the United States, President Macapagal felt secure in the mutual defense relationship. He was primarily concerned with maximizing American assistance in solving his economic problems. Without the United States, he saw no way out of his domestic difficulties.

In 1964 the air was still heavy with Philippine-American tensions on the eve of the incident at Tonkin Gulf. Aroused by the fatal shooting of Filipino trespassers at Clark Field, the air base north of Manila, leftist-organized demonstrators carried the usual "Yankee-go-home" placards and hanged the American ambassador in effigy. The need to cooperate in Vietnam relieved the escalating tensions. President Johnson orally accepted the Philippine contention that any armed attack against the Philippines would be regarded as an attack against the American forces stationed there and promised to step up American military aid. For his part, President Macapagal said that the pattern for the immediate future was clear—the historic and mutually beneficial Philippine-American partnership, as it related to Philippine security, economic progress, and freedom would continue. When Marcos came to power in 1965, the problems of nationalism were not solved; they were merely put on the back burner.

The intense period of Philippine nationalism that has just been described contains many useful lessons for those who would understand its future trends. Nationalists are neither pro-American nor anti-American. Such "pro-Americans" as Roxas and Magsaysay and such "anti-Americans" as Recto and Diokno are unfairly labeled. They may approve or disapprove of American policies, but they are fundamentally pro-Filipino. Nationalism is sincere, genuine, and not a mere front for journalists, commentators, writers, workers, teachers, and students who found a non-communist ideal they could cling to, or that they could exploit. But not all nationalists were genuine, as Teodoro Locsin, Sr. pointed out in an editorial in the *Philippines Free Press*:

In the barrios they do not understand a thing about nationalism. If nationalism would give the people in the barrios clothes, decent homes, adequate education, larger incomes, and a higher standard of living, then I would be all for it. But I have no use for those who keep saying they are nationalists but will not do a thing to help our masses live better. I am all for a positive, healthy nationalism which criticizes itself and recognizes our faults. We must broaden our horizons and not retreat into the distant past. We should sink our roots deep into the land of our fathers, but let the branches of our cultural tree seek light and sustenance wherever in the world they can be found.

Sentiments that Americans recognize as patriotism took deeper roots in the Filipino psyche, and they have not ceased to grow. Ambassador "Chip" Bohlen in 1959 observed that the nationalism then sweeping over the Philippines underscored that country's role as a friend and ally of the United States and a fearless foe of communism. "Any nation worth its salt must be animated by a spirit of active and vigorous nationalism," he said.

In thirty years, the nationalist movement has matured. Its xenophobic edges have been dulled and its power base enormously expanded. The danger is that the Filipinos' growing sense of pride in themselves will make them unreasonable in their demands. The hope is that they will see that extreme ultranationalism can be detrimental to their own interests in the contemporary interdependent world.

FOREIGN RELATIONS
UNDER MARCOS

The critics of President Marcos accuse him of having besmirched the image of the Philippine people abroad, but they must give him credit for his management of Philippine foreign relations. Behind him was the vision and the support of General Carlos P. Romulo, the nation's greatest diplomat-statesman. Romulo's distinguished career began at Corregidor, covered many years at the Philippine Embassy in Washington and the United Nations in New York, and ended as Marcos's minister of foreign affairs.

Philippine policymakers from Roxas to Marcos relied on the American relationship to bail them out of their difficulties and to promote their national interests. In dealing with both neighbors and distant nations, Philippine leaders were primarily concerned with keeping in step with the United States. This was not for the most part a painful process; their perceived interests were in harmony with the American outlook on the world. As Recto had said, the Philippines could always be counted upon to vote with the United States in the United Nations.

Marcos entered office feeling very good toward Americans because their aid to his "rice, roads, and schools" program had helped him win the election. In the hour of crisis in the Philippines that he described in his first inaugural address, he looked to the United States for help. The American involvement in Vietnam at that time worked to his advantage. In return for his cooperation and showing of the Philippine flag in Vietnam, he received from the United States the assistance he so desperately needed.

His first state visit to Washington in 1966 gave Marcos immeasurable political prestige at home and brought him forcefully to the attention of the American public. For the moment, U.S.-Philippine relations seemed as close as President Lyndon Johnson and Imelda Marcos as they danced around the ballroom floor at the White House. Marcos's visit won for the Philippines pledges of expanded assistance.

Within months after his triumphal return from Washington, Marcos convened the Manila Summit Conference of the heads of state and heads of government that had sent troops to Vietnam. He was projected into the limelight as a new leader of Southeast Asia. With American aid in his pocket, he played his dual role as chief executive and international statesman with consummate skill. Although completely identified with the United States, he never lost sight of the necessity for alternative Philippine policies should the United States tire of the Vietnam War and retreat to fortress America.

The Tet Offensive (1968) and the retirement of Lyndon Johnson by Richard Nixon on the American political scene stirred Marcos to action. He pulled his own men out of Vietnam and put Philippine diplomacy on a new and innovative basis. Based on the Filipino people's sense of their national identity and the ideals of the United Nations, his goal was to cater to the needs of economic and social development and to reduce the excessive reliance of the Philippines on the United States. The issue of nationalism, which had been in limbo for nearly a decade, was revived to become the most powerful weapon in the Marcos political arsenal. It was to be his best vote-getter in his bid for reelection.

As American embarrassments in Vietnam proliferated, Marcos distanced himself from the United States. He declared that the Mutual Defense Treaty should be revised in accordance with the old Recto formula, that the agreements on the bases should be reviewed, and special economic relations should be terminated. He adopted new policies to hedge his dependence on the United States. He launched a vigorous campaign to attract Japanese economic assistance. Before the United States began the switch from Taiwan to the People's Republic of China, Marcos made his own detente. He announced his intention to pursue an independent course of friendliness and openness toward socialist countries, even the Soviet Union. Turning to Southeast Asia, he worked successfully with Thailand, Malaysia, Singapore, and Indonesia to convert the moribund Association of Southeast Asia into a rejuvenated Association of Southeast Asian Nations (ASEAN). He would not reject ties with any country that sought ties with the Philippines.

As Marcos planned for martial law, he adopted a more complex, Machiavellian policy toward the United States. He could not abandon his nationalistic platform; neither could he accomplish his design for martial law without American assistance. Playing both ends against the middle, he continued to speak out against the nasty Americans, even as he conned Washington out of the weapons he needed to make martial law a success. Nothing increased anti-Americanism more in the Philippines than the obvious evidence that the United States aided and abetted Marcos in his rape of democracy, even though it was done in the name of law and order, anti-communism, and mutual security.

The vast changes in the balance of power in the western Pacific after the American exodus from Vietnam gave Marcos a great opportunity to sharpen his foreign policies. On May 23, 1975, he laid down his new guidelines for action:

> First, to intensify, along a broader field, our relations with the members of ASEAN.... Second, to pursue more vigorously the establishment of diplomatic relations with socialist states, in particular with the People's Republic of China and with the Soviet Union.... Third, to seek closer identification with the Third World, with whom we share similar problems.... Fourth, to continue our beneficial relationship with Japan.... Fifth, to support the Arab coun-

tries in their struggle for a just and enduring peace in the Middle East.... Finally, to find a new basis compatible with the emerging realities in Asia for a continuing, healthy relationship with the United States.

His actions implemented his own guidelines. In his speeches, he stressed that he was an Asian—Buddha, Jesus, and Gandhi were fellow Asians. He welcomed the expansion of trade with Japan and praised Japan for its substantial investments in a steel plant, a petroleum complex, a wood-processing plant, and sugar centrals. He expressed no objection to Japan's expanding military capability, but he was dubious about Japan's taking on the protection of the sea-lanes stretching 1,000 miles to the south, toward the shores of the Philippines. He normalized relations with all the socialist states, including the People's Republic of China and the Soviet Union.

In spite of his local arguments with Malaysia and Indonesia, he joined his ASEAN colleagues in supporting the Law of the Sea, the establishment of a zone of peace, freedom, and neutrality in Southeast Asia, and the recognition of the new states of Vietnam, Laos, and Kampuchea. In separate documents, the Philippines and Vietnam agreed that "neither would allow any foreign country to use each other's territory to launch aggression or to interfere with each other's affairs or with any country in the region," and that "they would settle peaceably any conflict between them, especially over the Spratly and Paracel Islands." The Philippines cooperated in the U.N.'s program for Vietnamese evacuees, but as a sop to Hanoi refused to offer asylum to any of the former Saigon officials.

Marcos was extremely active in the Middle East, largely because of his dependence on foreign oil. Beyond that, he was annoyed that the Arab states gave encouragement and support to the Muslim population in the southern Philippines. A half-million Filipino workers scattered from Libya and Saudi Arabia to Iraq and Kuwait commanded Marcos's serious attention because of the $1 billion annual earnings of precious foreign exchange.

President and Mrs. Marcos pointed with pride to their record in saving the country from the communists, preserving the sovereign independence of the Philippines, and enhancing its reputation in the world community. During their tenure in Malacañang, they associated the Philippines with the non-aligned states and the Third World. They put their country on record as supporting general and complete disarmament, endorsing nuclear non-proliferation, and opposing nuclear testing, especially in the Pacific. They continued to play a prominent role in the United Nations. In the beehive of diplomatic activity, the first lady was queen. She buzzed almost continuously from Manila to Peking, Moscow, Katmandu, Libya, Tehran, Rome, Paris, Washington, and New York. Her personal photograph album was a "Who's Who" of political celebrities and the international jet set.

A good deal of the Marcos diplomacy was shadowboxing. He could not dodge the stark fact that the Philippines, though sovereign and independent, was embarrassingly dependent on the United States. He could not ignore the United States; neither could he dance around it. For nearly fourteen years after the proclamation of martial law— through the administrations of Nixon, Ford, Carter, and Reagan— he played his cards with great skill. He succeeded in being known as America's friend, but never as "America's boy." He convinced his own people that in the U.S.-Philippine relationship, it was he who manipulated the United States rather than vice versa.

Sometimes he treated the United States with scorn: "You have done nothing for us except in your own interest"; sometimes with politeness: "I bring you a message of fraternal affection for the great American democracy that flourished in freedom and served as the trustee of civilization for all humanity"; and sometimes with threats: "If you do not pay us the rent we deserve for our bases, we will turn to someone who will." To his own people, his constant assurance was that he would cooperate with the United States only so long as cooperation would serve the Philippine interest.

For her part, Imelda was even more whimsical and contradictory than her husband. In her opinion, "You Americans do not understand how hard we worked for our people, how valuable we are to you. We are your most important allies and friends. We understand you better than you understand us. We are complex; you are so easy to see through. You are linear, interested only in decisions. We are multidimensional, interested in values and attitudes—heart, mind, and soul." In a cynical tone she added, "Your whole strategic position in the western Pacific depends upon the Philippines, yet you continue to treat us as your little brown cousins."

RENEGOTIATING
THE MILITARY BASES

Seeing the humiliating American exodus from Saigon as an advantage for the Philippines, Marcos believed the time was ripe for discussions on the military bases and military assistance. His goal, he said, was not blood money from the United States, but only military supplies as already promised, and a just rent in exchange for continued American use of the bases. After four years of intermittent negotiations, on January 7, 1979, a series of diplomatic exchanges of notes formalized the agreements that follow: It was reaffirmed that "the bases are *Philippine* military bases over which Philippine sovereignty extends." Each base will be under a Philippine commanding officer, but the United States shall have within these bases certain facilities and areas over which the United States shall have effective command and control, and unhampered operations. Only the Philippine flag shall fly over the bases, although on certain occasions and in certain places, the U.S. flag may be flown. The development of base lands to be relinquished by the Americans shall not interfere with the unhampered use of the bases. Noting the social and economic conditions around the bases, the two countries expressed a joint interest in developing programs to upgrade them. The Philippine government assumed responsibility for perimeter security of the bases. The entire agreement was to be reviewed every five years.

With respect to compensation for the use of the facilities, President Carter assured President Marcos that the American administration would make its best effort during the next five years (1980-1985) to obtain appropriations from the Congress for the Philippines of the following amounts of security assistance: military assistance, $50 million; foreign military sales credits, $250 million; and security supporting assistance, $200 million.

The first of the reviews was undertaken in the spring of 1983, with President Reagan in the White House, but before the assassination of Ninoy Aquino. Specific measures were agreed on to improve military operations centering on the bases: The United States would submit information on force levels and on their equipment and weapons systems in the Philippines, and would cooperate with the Philippine government in improving the social and economic conditions in Angeles City, Olongapo City, and other areas surrounding the bases. The bases labor agreement would be reviewed to increase the procurement of Philippine goods and services by the U.S. forces to the maximum extent possible.

The pledge of security assistance was increased to $900 million for the second five-year period: $125 million in grant military assistance, $300 million in foreign military sales credits, and $475 million in economic assistance. There is no provision for respective proportions in annual installments; only an overall sum for the entire period.

Meanwhile the Philippine economy skidded toward disaster, and Americans were directly affected. The bait that Marcos had offered to attract foreign loans and investments lost its lure. As the grasping, corrupt administration injected itself more and more into private business, investment in the Philippines lost its attraction. With the sky-rocketing cost of oil and the declining prices for Philippine exports, the American interest in Philippine trade declined. The staggering foreign debt ($26 billion) of the Philippine government was a warning signal of impending financial crisis. The course of wisdom for Americans as well as Filipinos seemed to be to get their money out of pesos into dollars, and, if possible, to transfer it out of the country.

REASSESSMENT
OF U.S. POLICY

With the turning of the tide of public opinion in the Philippines against Marcos and the manifest decline of confidence in his government in the beginning of the 1980s, Marcos had to face an unpleasant reality. He was an embarrassment to the United States. The fact that its aid was indeed the indispensable support of the Marcos dictatorship fueled the fires of growing anti-Americanism among the Filipino people.

The ink was scarcely dry on the Military Bases Agreement when the assassination of Ninoy Aquino occurred, all but destroying the last bit of American faith in President and Mrs. Marcos. A U.S. State Department spokesman condemned the murder as a cowardly and desperate act and expressed his trust that the government of the Philippines would bring the perpetrators to justice. Testifying at a congressional hearing, U.S. Assistant Secretary of State John Monjo said, "Many Filipinos suspect the complicity of the Philippine government in the crime."

Washington embarked on the difficult tasks of retaining the respect and friendship of the Filipino people, cooperating with an allied government, and distancing itself from President Marcos. President Reagan postponed his state visit to the Philippines, although he wrote a personal letter to President Marcos saying, "We have confidence in your ability to handle things." Observing the changes taking place in American policy, Marcos felt that he was being deserted by his friends in his time of travail and adjudged guilty without a trial. He complained of harassment by the liberal-tinged foreign media and warned the Americans that to replace or destroy him would open the doors to the communists. His bitterness against the United States simmered within him at precisely the same time that demonstrators in Manila paraded with their signs, "Marcos Resign" or "Out with the American Bases."

Much to Marcos's dismay, leading UNIDO opposition leader Doy Laurel was cordially received in Washington by Vice-President Bush and other dignitaries. Some policymakers in the United States publicly stated that it would be easier to support the Philippines if the Marcos government were to conduct a thorough, impartial, and swift investigation into Aquino's murder and hold a free, fair, and honest election for the National Assembly in May 1984. Americans kept sufficient aid flowing to honor their obligations and to prevent economic disaster, but not enough to underpin any grand design for economic recovery.

From the National Assembly elections of 1984 to the presidential election of February 1986, Marcos felt the growing pressure of American policy. Secretary of State Shultz, with Marcos in mind, told the world in general: "The United States seeks peace; we seek economic progress; we seek to promote freedom, democracy, and human rights.... It is now more and more widely recognized that there is a crucial connection among them." In Manila, Ambassador Stephen Bosworth repeatedly made similar statements to Filipino audiences. At each hearing on aid bills, the U.S. Congress expressed increasing doubts about the efficacy and advisability of further grants of military and economic support to the Philippines *under Marcos*.

Early in 1985 an inter-agency policy group in Washinton leaked to the press an official statement of policy that was, of course, read in Manila. American interests in the Philippines were defined as having the Philippines as a stable, democratically-oriented ally; unhampered access to our facilities at Subic Bay and Clark Field; a strong ASEAN, including a healthy Philippines; and a strong investment and trade position. Specific American objectives were divided into three categories.

Politically, the United States wished to see a credible conclusion to the Aquino trials and a peaceful transition to a succession government. It hoped for clean, fair, and honest elections in 1986 and 1987; for an end to presidential decree-making power in the Philippines; and for the revival of a Congress with legislative responsibility.

Economically, in the interest of social justice, the United States favored tax reform, more equitable extension of credit, and the dismantling of the crony monopolies. It would be pleased to see a more rapid movement away from government in business, and toward a market-oriented economy.

Militarily, the United States favored changes for the better in leadership and training of the armed forces, and in their treatment of civilians. It was willing to provide military assistance but not willing to support activities that tended to create more communists than they destroyed.

The American dilemma in dealing with the Philippines was accurately reflected in the congressional debates over military assistance. How could the United States justify any aid at all to the Philippines under present circumstances? How could it be made clear to the Filipino people that American aid is for them and not for the regime in power? What changes would have to take place in the Philippines to induce the Americans to make substantially larger grants? If Marcos were to remain in office, could any of the American objectives be achieved?

No mysteries shrouded U.S. policies, motives, or intentions with regard to the Philippines near the end of the Marcos administration. When Secretary Shultz was asked whether, in light of the growing opposition to the Marcos regime, the United States would continue to support Marcos, he replied: "Yes, he is the legitimate head of state and we will deal with him." Then he added, "We will also be working in every way that we can to help the Philippines legitimize all manner of processes—democratically-based procedures—through which their leadership should be chosen." But Marcos, and the opposition that was gearing for action, could appreciate the bottom line in the American position. The United States was not tied to Marcos or committed to any other particular leader. To protect American interests, it would cooperate with anyone whom the Filipinos elected.

9

"We are all Filipinos, whose
first duty is to be pro-Filipino, dedicated
to the principle that the
nation comes first, ahead of any personal
or partisan consideration."

President Aquino

FOREIGN RELATIONS: THE AQUINO SCENARIO

Although weighted down with massive domestic burdens, President Aquino is fully aware of the importance of foreign relations. She speaks for her nation in world affairs. Hers is the responsibility for preserving and enriching the historical record of her people, articulating their needs and goals, and defining and protecting their national interests. In addition to revitalizing their social values, reviving their democracy, rehabilitating their economy, and restoring law and order, the Filipinos, under her leadership, must regain the status in the world community to which they are entitled by their talents and capabilities.

A NEW APPROACH
TO FOREIGN AFFAIRS

While a candidate for the presidency, Cory stated her platform on foreign relations very succinctly:

> 1. To uphold the supremacy of our national interests in all our relations with other nation-states

2. To develop friendly relations with all nation-states and cease to be dependent on, or subordinate to, any other nation-state
3. To actively cooperate with our Asian neighbors to make Southeast Asia, in particular, a zone of neutrality, freedom, and peace—free of all nuclear weapons, and free from the domination of all foreign powers
4. To support the United Nations and all international organizations involved in the struggle for world peace and based on justice, and to join all organized efforts to curb the arms race, reduce the threat of nuclear war, and avoid confrontation that could lead to a nuclear holocaust
5. Subject to our rights under international law and to our fundamental right to national survival, we shall respect the U.S. military bases agreement up to 1991, when it expires. Since many events may occur between now and 1991, we shall keep all our options open
6. To re-examine and evaluate all arrangements and agreements entered into by the Marcos dictatorship from the standpoint of our national interest. Those that are against our national interests should be repudiated.

This statement is remarkable in that it refers three times to "national interest," once to the Marcos dictatorship, and only once to the United States—and only with reference to the specific issue of the military bases. Like everyone else in the Philippines of her generation or younger, she thinks first and foremost of what is good for the Philippines and not of what is good for the United States in the Philippines. She is going to reappraise the Marcos policies, keeping those she approves of and repudiating those that she judges to be detrimental. The most vexatious problem of all—the military bases—she postpones for future consideration. Her overriding concern is not the approval of the United States, but the security and welfare of her own nation in its dealings with *all* nation-states, regardless of ideology, geographic location, or military power.

Her intentions are easy to articulate but difficult to carry out. She cannot simply state her objectives and expect them to be accomplished. Her power is limited; she must deal with adversaries and allies at every step of the way. She must also respond to public opinion and to the demands of influential pressure groups within her own society. As she rides the crest of the wave of People Power, she benefits from her massive support at home and the unanimous acclaim of the free world. She is better known (thanks to television) and more praised in the United States than any other Filipino leader, including Quezon, Magsaysay, and Marcos, has ever been. But she must brace herself for possible changes. In standing firmly for what she believes to be right, she must anticipate conflicts with those whose perceptions of the national interest run counter to her own.

The team she has chosen to assist her in the conduct of foreign relations represents the best of Filipino talent and experience. Her vice-president, Doy Laurel, has been named minister of foreign affairs. Thoroughly at home in the United States, he is also experienced in dealing with Japan and the member states of ASEAN. To assist him in his ministry, he has appointed seasoned diplomats, including Joe Ingles, a former minister of foreign affairs, and Leticia Shahani, an expert on the United Nations and the Middle East. The new ambassador to the United States is Emmanuel (Manny) Pelaez, former vice-president of the Philippines, minister of foreign affairs, and member of the Philippine panel for negotiations on the military bases. A long-time associate of Pelaez, S.P. Lopez—a former ambassador to the United States, president of the University of the Philippines, journalist, and professor of English—has been sent to New York as ambassador to the United Nations.

The highly respected Alex Melchor, graduate of the U.S. Naval Academy, banker, industrialist, and former right-hand man to Marcos, has been "exiled" (with the blessing of Cardinal Jaime Sin) as ambassador to Moscow. Generals Ramos and Ileto, graduates of West Point, and hundreds of senior officers with advanced training in U.S. military schools can be helpful in handling American affairs. In Cory's cabinet is a thoroughgoing nationalist, Teodoro Locsin, Jr., who is intimately acquainted with Americans and American opinions.

President Aquino herself is probably the most knowledgeable of the lot about the United States, having spent her impressionable high-school and college years there. She returned to the U.S. to live in Boston from 1980 through 1983, where she spent with Ninoy and her family what she described as the happiest years of her life, thinking about and planning for their future in the Philippines. Whatever decisions she makes in foreign policy will be her own, but they will be based on consultations with, and the advice of, her team.

Many of the new president's decisions will inevitably reflect her reactions to the policies of former President Ferdinand Marcos. In speculating about what Marcos would have done in a given situation, she is inclined to do the opposite. It will not be easy to forget and forgive those, particularly in the United States, who supported Marcos in spite of his abandonment of democracy and his flagrant abuses of human rights. Most important in fashioning her policies will be the attitudes and convictions of a whole generation of Filipino leaders, of whom she herself is the outstanding example and the elected spokesperson. Her instinct is to reject what Marcos has done, but common sense tells her to retain the good. Her administration, and those that will come after her, are no more than tiny rivulets in the mainstream of Philippine history.

The revolution that propelled Cory Aquino into Malacañang gave her a mandate to fashion a new diplomacy as well as a new democracy. For more than twenty years Marcos, as the spokesman for the Philippine nation, was regarded abroad as "Mr. Philippines," the quintessential Filipino. During the first years of his administration, this was essentially detrimental to the image of the Filipino; in the latter years, as the graft and corruption associated with him became the scandal of the world, it was a disaster.

When Cory came to power, she completely reversed the image. Displacing the Marcos stereotype, *she* became the typical Filipino—representing courage, integrity, and morality. By her character and the trust she inspired she revolutionized the relations between the Philippines and the rest of the world. The nations dealing with the Philippines displayed a new willingness to be cooperative and helpful.

As heir to Quezon, Osmena, Magsaysay, Romulo, Recto, and Marcos, she could not scuttle the record of Philippine diplomacy. Old problems and traditional conflicts of interest would continue, but she would tackle them with a will and a spirit distinctly her own. She could be just as stubborn and nationalistic as any of her predecessors, but she would negotiate exclusively for the good of her country with no thought of personal glory.

WORKING WITH JAPAN
AND ASEAN

In her campaign speeches, Cory stressed that, once she was elected, concrete measures in matters of foreign policy would be granted second priority. First, she would concern herself with the purgation and purification of her government and the moral regeneration of her people. Having neither specific training nor any particular expertise in foreign affairs, she would venture into that area with great care. She asked for understanding and for patience.

For the Philippines the basic rule of diplomatic conduct is to maintain peaceful and friendly relations with all countries regardless of ideology. "At the same time," she said, "we shall revitalize our relations with our fellow member states in the ASEAN and we shall promote more balanced and suitable relations with the United States, Japan, the countries of Western Europe and the Pacific Basin, and all other countries with which we share a common loyalty to the principles of democracy."

As she sees it, foreign relations are not founded on prosaic formulas of diplomatic treaties, but on the dignity of each nation with the family of nations. "Twenty years ago," she said, "we enjoyed the respect of our neighbors and of the larger world community, but today we have largely lost that honor and respect." Then she continued:

> Before we can mend our international fences where they have been damaged and build bridges where there are none, before we can be accepted as friends and not suspected as swindlers, we must rebuild our confidence in ourselves as a nation. We cannot negotiate our foreign relations with dignity and honor, and we cannot build solid bridges of international friendship unless we can restore our self-respect as a nation... knowing that we are trusted because we are honest, respected because we are credible, eagerly sought because we are competent and because we are loyal to our pledged word.

She ventured slowly, as she had announced she would, into the arena of foreign affairs, maintaining an open mind on some of the dilemmas dividing her people. While she appreciated the necessity of a strong military establishment, she would not reject out-of-hand the idea of a neutral, nuclear-free zone in Southeast Asia. The ideal of non-alignment had its attractions, but it was impractical for the Philippines. She held to her faith in arms control and in the processes of the United Nations as steps toward universal peace and an eventual rule of law.

Soon after taking office, the new president received a stream of visitors: Secretaries Shultz and Weinberger from the United States, Prime Ministers David Lange and Bob Hawke from New Zealand and Australia, and Prime Minister Lee Kuan Yew from neighboring Singapore. All expressed delight in the way the new president of the Philippines conducted their discussions.

She immediately sent delegations abroad to clarify her position on economic affairs: She would honor accumulated debts but would seek restructuring for better terms, and she would welcome foreign assistance. Vice-President Laurel carried her message to Japan and to Western Europe. On her return from the United States in November, at the invitation of Prime Minister Nakasone, she herself paid a state visit to Japan in order to restore momentum to Philippine-Japan relations.

At the time President Aquino assumed office, negotiations in Tokyo on Japan's thirteenth international loan to the Philippines were stalled. The loan was for Y 49.5 billion*, of which Y 16.5 billion was to be in commodities and Y 33 billion was to be used to subsidize twelve projects, including roads, waterworks, and modernization of airport facilities. The Japanese Diet, like the American Congress, had become reluctant to continue its grants to Marcos because of the reported kickbacks and payoffs. With the new Philippine scenario in place, the Japanese wanted to resume the government's lending policies and to put their companies back in business in the Philippines. It was Cory's task to remove the roadblocks and to get the machinery moving.

The Japanese have substantial interests in the Philippines. Japan extends more official development loans to the Philippines than does the United States, and ranks second only to the United States in exports to the Philippines and in its cumulative investments there. The thirteen loans extended by Japan to the Philippines over the years amounted to Y 466 billion (more than $3 billion). In 1986, Japan had investments in 360 enterprises in the Philippines, compared with 658 in 1980. Japanese capital took flight, as other foreign investments did, with the deterioration of the Philippine political and economic situation. The Philippines stood to lose some very large investors. One trading company alone—Marubeni—is reported to have Y 7 billion of its own in a dozen joint ventures, including copper smelters, other mineral developments, and a variety of packaging and assembly

---

*Y = yen.

plants. Nine Japanese metropolitan banks, including Fuji, Mitsui, Mitsubishi, and the Bank of Tokyo, have regional branches or liaison offices in Manila. Such firms as Toyota, Nissan, and Isuzu among the automakers and Hitachi and Matsushita among the electronic manufacturers are ready to resume their suspended operations.

The Filipinos are aware that however eager Japan may be to move forward in the Philippines, they must be cautious. The clouds of World War II have not entirely disappeared. Not wishing to be used by the regional powers as a rival to the United States, the Japanese are careful to keep in constant touch with the Americans with respect to their security and economic assistance policies. Japan-Philippine relations, like U.S.-Philippine relations, are never conducted without serious consideration to the third side of the triangle, U.S.-Japan relations. Although dedicated to the common goal of mutual security in Southeast Asia, Japan and the Philippines have no political understandings such as a non-aggression pact or a mutual defense treaty. Japan is barred by its constitution from granting military assistance to any outside power.

Since the burden of military assistance to the Philippines consequently falls on the shoulders of the United States, it is only reasonable that Japan should absorb more of the costs of non-military economic assistance. Seeking to coordinate their policies, Japanese and Americans consult continuously with their Filipino counterparts on such matters as the kinds and amounts of assistance to be made available to the Philippines, types of technology to be transferred, terms for repayment of overdue debts, and respective policies to be pursued in such multilateral lending institutions as the World Bank, the IMF, and the Asia Development Bank. In her campaign promise, Cory said she would promote balanced and suitable relations with Japan; her visit to Japan was clearly a step in the right direction.

Although a member of the original Association of Southeast Asia (ASA, consisting of Thailand, Indonesia, and the Philippines) in 1960; of Maphilindo (Malaysia, the Philippines, and Indonesia) three years later; and the current ASEAN in 1967, the Philippines never enjoyed the full faith and confidence of its associated states. The Philippines had no need to pay for its own defense, to develop a coherent foreign policy, or to create a professional foreign service. Other ASEAN members always assumed that Uncle Sam was the "sugar daddy" who would come to the Philippines' rescue. It was a mark of disdain, especially in Indonesia, that the Philippines never had to fight to prove themselves worthy of independence. Unlike the other newly emerged states of Southeast Asia, the Philippines was handed its independence on a silver platter.

As long as Marcos was in power, the other member states of ASEAN were disinclined to take any position on Philippine affairs, convinced as they were that the United States would not let anything radical happen. No other Southeast Asian had any particular sympathy for either Marcos or the first lady. It was felt that Marcos, in his quarrels with Malaysia over Sabah and aid to the Muslim rebels, avoided reason in arguing the issues and resorted to posturing and name-calling. His support of ASEAN's majority views on Vietnam and Kampuchea was regarded as a matter of convenience rather than genuine concern. Imelda's spectacular safaris were dismissed as blatant exhibitionism, primarily designed to send a special message to the Americans.

Philippine relations with ASEAN were revolutionized in the new Aquino scenario. After the outburst of people power in the Philippines, Cory enjoyed prestige unrivaled by any leader in Southeast Asia, with the possible exception of Lee Kuan Yew, prime minister of Singapore. No longer could the Filipinos be accused of being immature. What Marcos could not accomplish by his imperious demeanor, Cory accomplished with quiet dignity. She was not an American puppet; anybody could see that, and she had no need to proclaim it. As president, in her first official trip abroad, to Indonesia and Singapore, she gave evidence of the high priority she attached to relations with her neighbors. By meeting face-to-face with their leaders, she would lay a firm foundation for future cooperation.

Her intention, as she explained, was to get acquainted; to explore issues, not to settle them. No doubt she tested her hosts with respect to Sabah and arms for the Muslim rebels, and discussed with them future relations with both Vietnam and Kampuchea. She was not gentle in referring to ASEAN itself. Pointing out that the organization was created to promote cultural and economic cooperation, she suggested that perhaps it was better not to talk about its failure. Rather than blame the outside world for ASEAN's lack of progress, she urged, "Let us get to work and help each other." She told a story: "A distinguished and respected friend, a former marine, gave me this advice—take care of your marines and they will take care of you.... And by the way, that friend was Secretary of State George Shultz."

No question burns more in the heart of ASEAN than the clash between American use of the military bases in the Philippines and the ultimate ideal of making Southeast Asia a zone of peace, freedom, and neutrality (ZOPFAN). The Philippines has taken a good deal of heat from its neighbors for allowing the American military presence on its soil. Each of them has insisted that it would never permit such a violation of the sovereignty of its homeland. All *openly* reject the argument that American bases contribute to regional security. They insist that no member state of ASEAN is in any danger from external aggression, and that in countering domestic insurgency, foreign bases are of no use at all. They argue further that the American facilities on the Philippine bases constitute an alien element in the Asian environment. At best, those facilities are temporary and they must go—otherwise ZOPFAN will never come into being.

Such reasoning as this represents only one horn of the dilemma. What most ASEAN members say openly is not what they say *in private*. In private they say, thank God for the American presence in our region—it is the only guarantee of peace that we have against the growing Soviet menace. In line with her continuing negotiations with the Americans, Cory needs to know exactly where her neighbors stand. Do they want the Yanks to go home, or don't they? If they want the Americans to leave, what alternatives can they come up with to provide for regional defense? If they want the Americans to stay, let them take the heat off the Philippines. If they wish to share in the benefits of American protection, it is only fair that they should pay their share of the costs.

RELATIONS WITH
THE UNITED STATES

Japan and her neighbors in ASEAN pose problems far less complicated than those the new president faces in dealing with the United States. The interests involved are more extensive, the roots of conflict deeper, the differences of opinion sharper, and the emotions more inflammable. President Reagan's priorities in the Philippines are American security and the protection of legitimate American interests; President Aquino's first concerns are a decent government, the welfare of the poor and the unemployed, and the moral regeneration of her people. What the United States wants from the Philippines is a stronger ally; what the Philippines wants from the United States is help in its national development.

The new president is aware of the love-hate sentiments that have always characterized Philippine-American relations. Young people still wear Harvard or Stanford T-shirts as they chant, "Yankee, Go Home." More Filipinos still gather in front of the American Embassy seeking visas than carry the placards denouncing the American bases. She has lived through it all. She has been exposed to the brilliant and bitter excoriation of "American imperialism" and it does not faze her. Next to the Philippines, the United States is the place where she feels most at home.

She has a deep understanding of the American people and the American government. She does not confuse the two. She knows too many Americans to be guilty of any such meaningless generality as "I like Americans" or "I don't like Americans." Some she likes, and some she would just as soon forget. She is as much at home among Americans as she is among her own people. She judges any American as she judges any Filipino—entirely on the basis of his or her individual merit. If she seems to be difficult in her negotiations with any American, it is not because of an inherent prejudice.

She is equally balanced in her view of the American government. She appreciates its limitations, especially now that she has assumed the highest responsibilities of her own government, and she understands the inevitability of frustration. She is learning about the conflicts between principles and possibilities, between desires and capabilities. Understanding the role of such conflicts in the formation of foreign policy, however, is not sufficient to make her forget or forgive the twenty-year American support of the Marcos regime. She is grateful for the new direction in American policy, but its depth and its permanence are as yet untested.

In the interim between President Aquino's election (February 7, 1986) and her inauguration (February 25), the members of her headquarters staff underwent violent shifts in their attitudes toward the United States. The response to President Reagan's first statement about "a lot of cheating on both sides" was "To hell with the Americans!" The Habib visit, the restrained attitudes of Ambassador Bosworth and his staff, the energetic support given Cory by American television, the revised statements from Washington, and the American compliance in getting Marcos out of the Philippines combined, however, to lift pro-Americanism to a new high.

Within two hours after the Marcos party left Malacañang, Secretary Shultz, in the briefing room at the White House, read a statement that was warmly received in Manila:

> With a peaceful transition to a new government of the Philippines, the United States extends recognition to this new government headed by President Aquino.
>
> We pay special tribute to her for her commitment to non-violence, which has earned the respect of all Americans.
>
> The new government has been produced by one of the most stirring and courageous examples of the democratic process in modern history. We honor the Filipino people.
>
> The United States stands ready, as always, to cooperate and assist the Philippines as the government of President Aquino engages the problems of economic development and national security.

In short order, Secretary Weinberger and Congressman Solarz visited Manila to bring assurances of military and economic assistance. Perhaps the visits came too quickly. It appeared that the Americans were overemphasizing the importance of the military, that they were too eager to plunge into Philippine internal affairs. Solarz, who had been the most outspoken opponent of aid to Marcos, became the most fervent champion of as much aid as possible to the Philippines under Aquino.

Speaking to a large audience at the University of the Philippines, Congressman Solarz expounded his personal views. Americans should help the Philippine government recover the resources that the Marcoses and their cronies stashed away in the United States. The United States should transport without delay the almost $200 million worth of economic aid awaiting shipment to the Philippines. The government of the Philippines, in conjunction with the United States and other donor countries, should immediately convene a working group to formulate a comprehensive plan for the economic revival of the Philippines. The United States and other nations in a position to help should commit themselves to a long-term, multi-lateral foreign assistance program (commonly referred to as a mini-Marshall Plan). Finally, the United States should provide surplus food commodities to alleviate the tragic malnutrition in some areas in the Philippines and should, if requested, provide additional military assistance as well.

THE U.S. SHIFTS
ITS STANCE

On May 16, 1986, Deputy Assistant Secretary of State John Monjo laid before the Congress a definitive statement of the new U.S. policy toward the Philippines. According to Monjo, the U.S. government will promote close relations with the Aquino government and support its efforts to restore democracy. The preservation of American security interests and vigorous American support of democratic reforms are mutually reinforcing elements of the same policy. The American goal is to help the Philippines by forging stronger links with the new generation of Filipino leaders, assisting in restoring economic prosperity, enhancing the effectiveness and professionalism of the NAFP, and maintaining a continued close defense relationship with the Philippines. The American government believes that its security relationship will be strongest with an independent, democratic, and stable Philippines.

In a single year the American policy had dramatically reversed itself! The policy statement of February 1985, so cautiously leaked to the press, was negative and restrictive, pressuring Marcos to bring about needed reforms as the price of continued American aid. The statement of May 1986 was positive and helpful.

As for contributing to stability in the Philippines, Monjo told the Congress that President Aquino was committed to an economic program that Americans thoroughly approved. The success of that program would depend primarily on the efforts of the Filipinos, but the United States and the Philippines together had worked out an aid package geared to Philippine needs and priorities. The United States hoped that its aid would make substantial contributions in health, education, and agricultural sectors, and would reduce deficits in the budget and in the current international income account.

Speaking for the administration, Monjo asked for substantially increased assistance appropriations for fiscal year 1986. He asked that a total of about $500 million of economic assistance and $100 million in military assistance be made available to the Philippines between October 1985 and October 1986. More than 90 percent of this should be on a grant basis so as not to aggravate the heavy external debt problem of the Philippines.

President Aquino surrounded by members of Congress after her speech to a joint congressional meeting September 18, 1986. From left are: Senate Majority Leader Robert Dole of Kansas, House Minority Whip Trent Lott of Mississippi, and Rep. Lynn Martin, R-Illinois.

Monjo also told the Congress that the U.S. administration was taking measures in the trade and investment fields to help invigorate the private sector in the Philippines. These include new agreements with the Philippines on the Generalized System Preference (preferences granted to one Third World country will be granted to all), on textile quotas, and on expanded involvement by the U.S. Export-Import Bank and the Overseas Private Investment Corporation. According to Monjo, the United States was at one with other donor nations, multilateral lending institutions, and private sector international banks in seeking to assist the Philippine government in revitalizing the nation's economy.

It was one thing for the administration to present a program to Congress, and quite another to get it approved. In 1985, when the distribution of American aid in the Philippines was subject to the whims of President and Mrs. Marcos, the U.S. Congress was inclined to be tighter fisted. With Cory in power in 1986, its attitude changed. In spite of the atmosphere of Gramm-Rudman, the mountainous federal deficit, and the other burdens of the American taxpayers, the Congress, like the people it represented, was in a mood to be generous to the Philippines.

President Aquino's visit to the United States in September provided the impetus the Congress needed to finance the administration's program. Her simplicity contrasted so sharply with the Marcos flamboyance. That any woman—let alone a TV personality who was at the same time the president of her country—could pack into two suitcases the clothes she needed for continuous appearances before the cameras and for twenty-one public speeches in ten days—amazed her hosts. She struck just the right note with the Americans—relaxed, poised, humble—but always serious and dignified. Those who worried about her stand on the communists she asked for patience and understanding. Although she reaffirmed her belief that everyone, including the communists, should have the right to vote, and that the Communist Party of the Philippines should be legalized, she denied any intention of taking communists into her government. As for her policy toward the insurgents, she said, "Let it be clear to all who seek to overthrow our democratic government, dismantle our sacred democratic institutions, our cherished values, our fundamental belief in God, that I will not hesitate to fight them with all the resources of the republic should they refuse to lay down their arms." Small wonder that she was chosen by *Time* magazine as the woman of the year!

U.S. ECONOMIC AND
MILITARY ASSISTANCE

Filipinos generally appreciated American economic aid, although some grumbling could be heard in Manila. Some said, "Too little and too late"; others said, "We would sooner have your investments and loans." Some still looked upon American AID and Food For Peace, along with the USIA (United States Information Agency) and the Central Intelligence Agency (CIA), as overt or covert agents of the meddling U.S. government. Joker Arroyo, the chief cabinet secretary, on receiving a check for $200 million from Secretary Shultz, later commented: "Before we react with joy like jumping chimpanzees, remember this is not 'aid' money; it is money due us for the rent of our bases." To President Aquino, receiving aid is no affront to her dignity. Her people need all the help they can get.

Philippine-American accord on military assistance has been more difficult to reach. "Military assistance," including sales, loans, and grants, covers arms and ammunition, weapon systems, planes, ships, armored personnel carriers, armored trucks, and helicopter gunships. As part of the military assistance program, JUSMAG (Joint U.S. Military Advisory Group) works with the AFP in matters of strategic staff direction, logistics, training, and operational assistance. "Security-Support Assistance" consists of such non-lethal items as transport helicopters, jeeps, trucks, communications equipment, uniforms, combat boots, and training for police and riot control. Military assistance and security support assistance programs have made the AFP a clone of the U.S. armed forces.

To the Americans, the purpose of military assistance is to "assist friendly governments to defend themselves against threats to the national security of the United States; provide access to governments with whom the United States must interact; and maintain influence with the armed forces of the recipient country." To Marcos, U.S. military assistance was a means of developing his armed forces as a counter to insurgency and as an instrument of government to implement his decrees. Even under Marcos, questions arose about the benefits of military assistance. As an opposition leader said: "When the people see Filipino soldiers, with U.S.-supplied helicopters, guns, ammunition, and uniforms, shooting at Filipinos demonstrating against a repressive regime, one can expect a rise in anti-U.S. sentiment. The communists could not ask for a better propaganda tool."

President Aquino has her own ideas about military assistance. She is not anti-military, but she does not want *her* military tied so intimately to the Americans. She wants only such weapons and equipment as she deems necessary to counter the insurgents in *her* way, not the American way. She differs from the Americans in perception of the role of the military in the enforcement of law and order. As Cardinal Sin said, "We need subsidies, but not in the form of weapons. Bullets are no answer to economic inequities, social tensions, or political abuse."

In her view, the insurgents in the Philippines are not a threat to the national security of the United States, nor is military assistance necessary as a means of access to her government or for maintaining influence with her armed forces. Thus she denies the basic premises on which the Americans rest their military assistance program. Nor does she see any justification for the American contention that there is imminent danger of losing the Philippines to communism. She does not think that the armed bands of the NPA are warriors fighting for a set of principles or a coherent economic theory. They know what they are protesting *against*; they are hazy in what they are fighting *for*. Not many people in the Philippines believe that the communist insurgency is, as one person phrased it, "a part of the worldwide joust between the knights of the KGB and the Pooh Bahs of the Potomac."

She takes issue with many of her advisers who, after less than a year in office, argue that with the new training and the new reforms, the Philippine military will destroy the NPA. Her sharpest differences of opinion, however, are with the professional "freedom fighters" in Washington. She is not inclined to follow their advice in countering the communists. She tends to think that the Philippines can learn more about unconventional warfare from the Indonesians or the Thais than from the CIA or ex-Green Berets. She does not intend to let the Philippines become like Vietnam yesterday or Nicaragua today.

Some Americans, like President Reagan himself, have cautioned President Aquino that her policies are dangerous: The communists are expanding their areas of operations and increasing their terrorism; to try to negotiate with them is useless; armed struggle is their life blood and they will never give up. The only way to handle them is to strengthen the armed forces. American advice is to accomplish the military reforms that are needed, follow American counter-insurgency methods, and purchase more American arms through a generous military assistance program.

President Aquino says "No." She has no need of the quantities and types of weapons that the Americans want to sell her. She wants her soldiers to fight the communists in a Philippine, not an American, way. Vietnam proved that victory, even in a military sense, cannot be won by expensive weapons and sophisticated tactics alone. She would cut down drastically on the military assistance to be bought from the United States and paid for by the Philippines.

THE MILITARY
BASES

Filipino Views. President Aquino is just as firm in her views about the American facilities on the Philippine bases as she is in her views about military assistance. This is her forthright position:

> Concerning the military bases, let me simply reiterate the assurance I have already given that we do not propose to renounce the existing Military Bases Agreement or the Treaty of Mutual Defense with the United States. At the same time, however, I must state with candor that no sovereign nation should consent that a portion of its territory be a perpetual possession of a foreign power. The Bases Agreement expires in 1991. Before such date, a process of consultation will be undertaken—with the United States, with neighboring states, but above all, with the Filipino people—so that an arrangement that will serve the best interests of the entire free world, but especially of the Filipino people, can be reached.

Consultations with her neighbors have already been initiated, and consultations with her own people, on an informal and continuing basis, take place every day in anticipation of the review of the Military Bases Agreement (MBA), which is scheduled to begin before 1988. Actual negotiations with the Americans, not only on the MBA but on the entire security relationship between the Philippines and the United States, are likely to be long and difficult. Sharp differences divide the Americans and the Filipinos on the role and the value of the bases in mutual security. More importantly, the Filipinos differ among themselves with respect to the policy they should adopt toward the Americans.

Most Americans are convinced that the bases are of great value in guaranteeing peace, stability, and prosperity in the region of Southeast Asia and in projecting U.S. military power in its global confrontation with the USSR. Two-thirds of American supplies to Diego Garcia in the Indian Ocean pass through Clark Field; the Seventh Fleet could not carry out its mission in the Pacific-Asian area without Subic Bay Naval Base. American policymakers must be prepared to adjust to modifications in the MBA, but they are concerned that loss of those bases would be disastrous to American interests.

Americans in the Philippines do not think that Filipinos in their hearts oppose the bases as much as public opinion there would indicate. Most Filipinos appreciate the American presence; they admit the real and growing value of the bases to the Philippine economy. In a secret ballot, the "yes" vote for the bases would surely win. In view of the prevailing nationalistic mood, however, it would be political suicide for any Filipino to underscore the advantages to the Philippines of the continued unhampered American access to its facilities on the Philippine bases.

The consensus of Filipino opinion is that, not immediately but eventually, the bases will have to go. The Church is divided on the issue. Kit Tatad, a former cabinet minister and influential journalist, insists that the bases issue is not important to anybody except government officials and the residents of Olangapo and Angeles City. Ambitious leftist politicians and the more flamboyant of the media beat out the constant theme that the bases must go. Former cabinet ministers Salonga, Pimentel, Sanchez, Arroyo, and Saguisag are on record for the removal of the bases. On alternate days, Teddy Locsin, Jr. seems to be with them. Senator Tanada is a leader in the Anti-Bases Coalition (ABC), linking its position with the worldwide nuclear protest movement. The communists and their allies in the National Democratic Front are uncompromisingly anti-bases.

The Filipinos recite a litany of objections to the bases, some as old as the independent Philippine Republic and some with a distinctly contemporary flavor. The ABC still contends that "the bases impair our national sovereignty and independence, deprive our people of the full use and control of our national patrimony, support U.S. intervention in our internal affairs, and serve as staging grounds for gunboat diplomacy and intervention in the internal affairs of others." The old argument that the bases contribute to the degradation of moral values of the Filipino people is still extant, but new stress is laid on the dangers inherent in being indissolubly linked to American security policies.

Filipinos have their own interpretation of U.S. global objectives. One hears with increasing frequency that the bases are no longer defensive in nature, but offensive, being launching pads for aggression halfway around the world. Since Vietnam, there has been no change in American power or American policy. The only change has been in American methods. It is alleged that the bases are instruments of imperialism and domination, not equality and justice for all nations.

Growing numbers of Filipinos argue that from the beginning the primary concern of the U.S. has been unhampered access to their military facilities and not justice, freedom, and democracy for the Philippines. To them, "The American policy of altruism is a myth." They also argue that, given the amount of their payment for the use of the bases, the Americans are getting a comparatively free ride: "Spain, Greece, and Turkey get more than we do, and they are not saddled with special relations." The Americans allegedly pay $3 billion for landing rights in Israel, $2 billion for rights in Egypt, $974 million for the use of bases in Turkey, and $415 million for its bases in Spain. In contrast, the Philippines receives $180 million per year, with half of that in loans for military purchases. The irony is that the American installations in the Philippines are the largest and most strategic in the world. Filipinos suggest that $1 billion down payment and $1 billion a year cash would be a reasonable rent.

Labor troubles are not unknown on the Philippine bases. Although the workers are paid handsomely compared with workers elsewhere in the Philippines, they are poorly paid in comparison with their American counterparts. The last time the workers went on strike, their picket line was disrupted by protesting bar girls from the neighboring sailor town. Ladies of the night, carrying their own placards, said they did not want left-wing union leaders on the base depriving them of their livelihood.

For Filipinos the most worrisome issue about the bases is the danger of becoming victims of a nuclear holocaust. The bases are said to be the biggest storehouse of nuclear weapons in the Pacific area. The Filipinos understandably fear that this may make them a target of nuclear attack, or may involve them in a superpower nuclear war. One writer commented, "A computer error or miscalculation could trigger off a nuclear explosion, where 53 million Filipinos might perish without ever knowing why." Another wrote, "When the missiles fall on U.S. bases, no American general will return to liberate us from a nuclear fall-out." The anti-nuclear forces in the Philippines were strengthened by New Zealand's defiance of the U.S. nuclear ship policy. They are now watching closely to see if Japan will tighten the enforcement of its three nuclear principles: no manufacture, no entry, and no storage of nuclear weapons.

At least in some quarters in the Philippines the opinion that the bases are of diminished value to the nation is taking hold. "We do not need the bases, we have no use for them. We are in no danger of aggression from the outside, either from the Soviet Union, China, or a rearmed Japan. The bases do not really defend us or our neighbors. They do not tie Filipinos and Americans closer together, because the frequent incidents only exacerbate hard feelings. If goodwill is more important than bases, then it is conceivable that the bases will have to go. Bases cannot serve their purpose in a hostile environment." In the same vein, many Filipinos continue: "Do not worry about the losses if the bases go; the lands and resources could be converted into useful civilian assets dedicated to our national development. The income from the bases is a paltry sum compared to the billions of dollars of profits the U.S. companies are extracting from the Philippines. The social costs of national dignity are irreplaceable." Sound or not, these are the arguments they offer.

Filipinos with official responsibility cannot be so cavalier in their attitudes. It is one thing to proclaim ideals; it is quite another to raise the money to meet the government's budget. Policymakers are far more restrained than media or academic critics in planning for the future. They are aware of the dangers confronting the Philippines and of the benefits derived from the American connection. They, too, want complete control of their own destiny, but they insist that an agreement freely entered into is not a violation of their sovereignty. Not too eager to do away with the bases, they are more inclined to enter into an agreement extending beyond the year 1991 that will both protect the Philippine national interest and permit the Americans to use their facilities in the implementation of their global and defense strategies. Again, all that President Aquino has promised is that she will keep her options open.

Ambassador Pelaez sums up the Philippine situation by stating that there is no meeting of the minds on the storage of nuclear weapons, the use of the bases as missile-launching sites, criminal jurisdiction over military personnel, the actual limits on U.S. extraterritorial rights, or the nature and amount of U.S. compensation. He has said that unless the question of sovereignty over the bases is directly addressed and resolved in favor of the Filipinos, the clash in viewpoints will never cease. Ultimately, the Filipinos demand complete control over the bases so that they can put them to more advantageous and productive use.

Ambassador Lopez, in a more practical vein, argues: "Let us not be in a hurry to lose the American money; let us wait to see what the Russians do in Danang and Camranh Bay." Vice-President Laurel declined to go on record for removal of the bases, even though he insists on a completely independent foreign policy. He cautiously states, "We must not let the bases prevent the growth of our friendship and solidarity with other peoples, or prevent us from taking concrete measures looking toward a Zone of Peace, Freedom, and Neutrality and toward nuclear disarmament."

Current Differences. The shifts in attitude on the part of former Minister of Defense Enrile regarding the bases reflect the ambivalence in the thinking of Philippine officials. As a member of the Marcos establishment at the time the United States was threatening to reduce its military assistance, Enrile said the Philippines should abrogate the bases agreement. With the advent of President Aquino, Enrile changed his tune. "We need the bases as a permanent part of our defense," he said, "but we do not intend to rely on them forever." He acknowledged that the bases were vital to a balance of power in Asia and the Pacific as well as to the protection of the airways and sea-lanes in the region of the Southwest Pacific and the Indian Ocean. After his dismissal from Cory's cabinet (with U.S. approval) he returned to his old theme that the bases would have to go.

The confusion among Filipinos about the future of the bases was reflected in the proceedings of the constitutional convention. Some delegates wanted to insert a provision covering the bases in the new constitution; others preferred to leave the matter to the president and the legislature. Half a dozen resolutions were introduced, but none committed the Philippines to a categorical stand. One proposed that the bases agreement should extend beyond 1991, another that no foreign facilities should be permitted on Philippine soil after that date. Neither resolution passed. As noted above, the Constitution merely provides that, "consistent with the national interest, the Philippines pursues and adopts a policy of freedom from nuclear weapons," and that after 1991 "foreign military bases, troops, or facilities shall not be allowed in the Philippines except under a treaty duly concurred by a majority of the vote cast by the people in a national referendum held for that purpose, and recognized as a treaty by the other contracting state."

The most reasonable analysis of the Philippine national interest in the bases that I have encountered was written by Jerry Barican in the weekend edition of *Veritas*, January 13, 1985. In commenting on the platform of Marcos's united opposition, he wrote:

Finally, there is the call for the removal of the U.S. bases in the Philippines. It is the tragedy of political leaders that they often come to the right conclusions a generation too late. Those bases should never have been put or kept there in the forties, fifties, and sixties. But we are living in the world of the eighties, not in Recto's time. In the light of present conditions, it may be time to rethink our position on the bases.

As Afghanistan and Russia's support for Vietnamese expansion into Kampuchea show, the Soviet Union is not merely a nuclear, but a conventional power keen on projecting its influence. In the sixties, the Soviets did not have a base in Vietnam or a fleet in the South China Sea. They do now. Until we can persuade the two superpowers to leave the area militarily and convert Southeast Asia to a zone of peace and neutrality, it would not appear wise to unilaterally force the U.S. to abandon its presence in our region. The U.S. bases should never have been put here in the absence of a Soviet presence. They should not now be abandoned in the absence of a Soviet withdrawal and a commitment by both superpowers to leave our zone alone.

Barican argued that the nuclear magnet theory had validity in the fifties, when there were a total of only 2,000 nuclear warheads in existence. With arsenals of 50,000 warheads, the whole world is a magnet. He proposed that rather than removing the bases, they be relocated to a new and more distant site, in Palawan, for example. In exchange for a renewable ten-year lease, the Philippines could require an up-front payment of at least $2 billion. He said, "We may have reached the point of having to choose between social and economic peace with the bases, or no bases with a continuing crisis." In his view, "Our economic crisis is real and present, the danger of the bases' presence contingent and more distant. People are hungry and jobless now; the administration needs money. Fortunately, the U.S. has a strategic and geopolitical interest in the survival of a democratic Philippines. We can accommodate both interests in the light of our needs."

The ambivalence over the future of the bases is indicative of the uncertainty among thoughtful Filipinos—not the communists or the left-wing extremists—about the future of the entire security relationship between the Philippines and the United States. The ghosts of special relations continue to haunt them. Many still see their country as the captive of a superpower, shackled to an unequal relationship from which it has struggled in vain to escape. This is the image that prevails in the social science classes of almost any Philippine university. A new generation of leaders, the third since the Treaty of Paris, wishes to break the grip of the traditional oligarchies on foreign policy and to re-examine all the Philippine-American covenants of the past.

Doubts still exist about the genuineness of American assurances and the effectiveness of the American pledge of assistance in the event of external aggression against the Philippines. The doubts so firmly implanted by Recto's rhetorical elegance still rankle Filipino nationalists. The security guarantees of the Mutual Defense Treaty have never been considered adequate, especially since the American debacle in Vietnam. If the bases are to continue beyond 1991—so says no less a Philippine spokesman than Ambassador Pelaez—an entirely new treaty system will have to come into existence. A new treaty governing the use of the bases and a new Mutual Defense Treaty will have to be negotiated, ratified by the U.S. Senate and the Philippine Legislature, and submitted to the Philippine people in a national referendum. Pelaez says the old agreements are like an old house that its owners have tried to remodel over the years. Despite numerous repairs, it remains unsatisfactory. It would be better to tear it down completely and build a new one—if there is continued need for it.

Ambassador Pelaez is, of course, aware of the obstacles in the path he would like to pursue. Americans, too, have their ideas about the future. It may not be in the American interest to put security relations on a more binding basis than they are at present. Just as Filipinos do not want to be drawn into a possible U.S.-U.S.S.R. conflict beyond their immediate concerns, so Americans do not wish to be drawn into the Philippines' insurgency problems, its difficult relations with Malaysia over Sabah, or the frictions around the Spratly Islands. If the wording of the existing Mutual Defense Treaty seems vague, it is deliberately so. Anything more precise would have perished in the U.S. Senate and would probably meet the same fate today.

Filipinos can be expected to present their points of view as forcefully as possible, but they must know that the Americans will do the same. On January 1, 1979, an editorial in the *New York Times* stated an American point of view very clearly:

No country should imagine that it is doing the United States a favor by remaining in alliance with us.... No ally can pressure us by a threat of termination; we will not accept that its security is more important to us than it is to itself.... We assume that our friends regard their ties to us as serving their own national purposes, not as privileges to be granted or withdrawn as a means of pressure.

THE ROAD
AHEAD

Since the turn of the century, the United States has loomed large in the Philippine story, and it will continue to do so in the years ahead. There has never been a time—and it is safe to assume there never will be—when the nature of the U.S.-Philippines relationship has not aroused criticism. The seeds of hatred are particularly deep in the hearts of young people who, in their past twenty years, have seen the United States only as the supporter of the Marcos dictatorship.

Let the record speak for itself. Of course the Americans have looked after their own interests, but in the process they have left their mark on the Philippines. At the beginning of 1987, some 70,000 Americans resided in the Philippines, among them 14,000 service personnel, 4,000 Peace Corps volunteers, and 1,000 Roman Catholic priests. American investors—not the American government—have a $3 billion stake in the Philippines. Of the top fifty companies in the Philippines, ten are American owned. Some 34,000 Filipinos who served as navy stewards or in other military jobs received veterans' benefits through the American Embassy. More than a million Filipinos make their home in the United States, and still they come—at a rate of 40,000 to 50,000 per year. These personal ties are the best guarantee that the reservoir of goodwill can never run dry.

The love-hate relationship between Filipinos and Americans is bound to continue. Filipinos are hooked on American products and the American way of life, not because they are American but because they like them. The envy and the frustration experienced by the Filipinos in chasing after things American feeds their nationalism, which is stronger than ever. A strong nationalism is a healthy sign, and not one to be feared by the United States. As Ambassador Bosworth has observed, all the Americans require to deal with this nationalism is mutual respect and a lot of patience and sensitivity. As he put it, "We have handled it well in the past and we have every reason to continue to do so." Whatever their differences, cooperation between the Philippines and the United States is in their mutual interest, and both nations know it.

No matter how great the American role in the Philippines, the destiny of their country is in the hands of the Filipinos themselves. "People Power" made the year 1986 one of the proudest in their history, and thrust into leadership one of the most remarkable persons of their race. After little more than a year in office, she has given the nation a fresh start in political, economic, and military reforms and made an immeasurable impact on the moral regeneration of her people. She has discarded the yellow dress of the campaign trail and wrapped herself in the multi-colored mantle of her distinguished office. She faced Nur Misuari with the same unassuming courage with which she confronted President Marcos, and she met President Reagan with the same grace and dignity that she displayed before the Filipino people on her inauguration day.

She, and the Filipino people, have a rough road ahead. A change of government has not solved all the country's problems. The fact is that the struggle is just beginning. The stakes are enormous, and the outcome is still in doubt. It is far too early for celebration or self-congratulations. It is time for hard work, for help, and for good-will. I am reminded of Edmund Burke, who wrote in the eighteenth century:

> I should therefore suspend my congratulations on the liberty of France until I was informed as to how it had been combined with government, with public force, with discipline, with obedience of armies, with the collection and effectiveness of a well-distributed revenue, with morality and religion, with solidity and property, with peace and order, with civil and social manners. All these are good things too. Without them, liberty is of no benefit whilst it lasts and is not likely long to continue.

President Aquino's challenge is to keep her momentum going. She cannot be deterred by those to the left of her who charge that she still plays the game of the traditional oligarchs and dances to Washington's tune, or by those to the right of her who fear that she is gambling with the nation's future in playing too close to the communists. She says that she is enjoying her job, every minute of it, but it is wearing. Wryly she confesses, "It is more exciting to be a grandmother."

She herself has expressed her candid view of where she and her country stand in the contemporary world: "We are all Filipinos, whose first duty is to be pro-Filipino, dedicated to the principle that the nation comes first, ahead of any personal or partisan consideration." Looking to the past, she states, "We are an Asian nation, and thus heir to the rich cultural heritage of this ancient part of the world. At the same time, we are also heir to the religious heritage of Christianity and Islam, and beneficiaries of the great humanitarian values of Western democracy." Voicing the perplexities of every Filipino, she confesses, "It is true that there are times when our Asian cultural antecedents clash with our Western cultural legacy and threaten to fragment our cultural identity. It is also true that we are in many ways still in search of ourselves." She concludes her soliloquy on an upbeat note: "I am confident, however, that we can merge our rich but diverse heritage into a unified consciousness and tradition that we can truly call a Filipino culture. From this consciousness and tradition, we should be able to reach to the world not just from the pragmatic concerns of economics and politics, but also from a common heritage of shared moral and cultural values."

The story of Cory Aquino and the people of the Philippines continues. The chapter just concluded began in tragedy, with the blood-stained body of a martyr lying prone on the tarmac at the Manila airport. The drama intensified with the rising tide of revolt against a ruthless but aging ruler. The spectacular climax came when a human barricade halted the advancing tanks, when soldiers saluted the sign of the cross, when a sea of yellow tossed up a new national heroine, and when history once again revealed the vulnerability of a posturing dictator. Most memorable of all was the happiness, the sheer joy, the laughter and tears that abounded as millions of people shouted to the heavens, "We are free."

A new chapter has begun. A remarkable person has assumed the presidency. Americans have seen an unassuming person, inspired by memories, courage, and faith in God and democracy, become a world-class leader. The sobering reality is that she is submerged in the mass of problems that constitute the Marcos legacy. The frenzied days and nights of the people's revolution have given way to a sober reality. Reflecting the current mood in the Philippines, a Filipino friend recently said to me, "We are down, but we are destined to play an important role in the coming 'Age of the Pacific.' We have a rendezvous with the twenty-first century that we must hasten to keep." If they add a generous amount of hard work and social discipline to their spiritual qualities and their love of life, there is a good chance that the rendezvous will be a happy one.

SUGGESTED READING

These bibliographical notes are intended to indicate some of my most useful sources and to serve as a guide for further reading.

In trying to keep up with events in the Philippines, I follow closely the *Asian Survey*, the *Asian Wall Street Journal*, the *Christian Science Monitor*, the *Far Eastern Economic Review*, the *New York Times*, and the *Philippine News of San Francisco*. Through the years in the Philippines, I have been a constant reader of the *Free Press* and the magazine *Solidarity*.

A few current magazine articles have more than a passing value. Among these are:

Buss, Claude. "Waking from a Dream." *Wilson Quarterly*, Summer 1986.

Kessler, Richard J. "Policy Paper 37" in *U.S. Policy Toward the Philippines After Marcos*. Muscatine, Iowa: The Stanley Foundation, 1986.

Manning, Robert. "The Philippines in Crisis." *Foreign Affairs*, Winter 1984/1985.

Miller, Stuart Creighton. "Compradore Colonialism." *Wilson Quarterly*, Summer 1986.

Munro, Ross H. "The New Khmer Rouge." *Commentary*, December 1985.

Shaplen, Robert. "A Reporter at Large" (Letter from Manila). *The New Yorker*, August 25, 1986, and September 1, 1986.

Zich, Arthur. "Hope and Danger in the Philippines." *National Geographic*, July 1986.

————. "The Marcos Era." *Wilson Quarterly*, Summer 1986.

Students of Philippine affairs benefit from the constant flow of policy statements made by U.S. officials. These are obtainable in the United States from the Bureau of Public Affairs in the State Department, and in Manila from the U.S. Information Service at the American Embassy. The published hearings of the appropriate committees of the U.S. Senate and the House of Representatives, as well as special studies and situation reports, are invaluable sources of information.

At international conferences on Asian affairs and/or security issues held all over the world, valuable papers on the Philippines are often presented that deserve a wider popular audience. Professional magazines and various concerned private organizations frequently present analyses of specific Philippine problems. Among the authors deserving careful attention are Karl Jackson, Larry Niksch, Marjorie Niehaus, Carl Lande, Lela Noble, Guy Pauker, James Gregor, David Wurfel, Caroline Hernandez, and Jesus Estanislao.

For coverage of the events of 1986, I especially recommend Mercado Monina Allarey, *People Power: The Philippine Revolution of 1986,* preface and scenarios by Francisco S. Tatad (Manila: James B. Reuter, S.J. Foundation, 1986) and *Bayan Ko* (My Country), written by Guy Sacerdoti and Lin Neumann and illustrated by a team of the world's greatest photojournalists, headed by Carl Mydans. These are coffee-table books: The stories are sound and the pictures are spectacular. I urge you to be on the lookout for Stanley Karnow's television series on the United States and the Philippines.

I hope the following list is helpful.

Abella, Domingo. *From Indio to Filipino.* Manila, Philippines: De La Salle University Press, 1978.

Agoncillo, Teodoro and Milagros C. Guerrero. *History of the Filipino People.* 5th ed. Quezon City, Philippines: R. P. Garcia Publishing Co., 1983.

Apostol, Eugenia D., ed. *Reports of the Fact Finding Board on the Assassination of Senator Benigno S. Aquino, Jr.* Manila: Mr. and Ms. Publishing Co., 1984.

Avanceña, Rose Laurel, and Ilena Maramag. *Days of Courage: The Legacy of Dr. Jose P. Laurel.* Manila: (Published privately), 1980.

Bain, David Howard. *Sitting in Darkness: Americans in the Philippines.* Boston: Houghton-Mifflin, 1984.

Bresnan, John, ed. *Crisis in the Philippines: The Marcos Era and Beyond.* Princeton, N.J.: Princeton University Press, 1986.

Bunge, Frederica M. *The Philippines: A Country Study.* U.S. Army Area Handbook Series. Washington, D.C.: Government Printing Office, 1984.

Buss, Claude A. *United States and the Philippines: Background for Policy.* Washington, D.C.: American Enterprise Institute and the Hoover Institution Policy Study, 1977.

Canoy, Reuben R. *Counterfeit Revolution.* Manila: Philippine Editions Publishing, 1984.

Constantino, Renato. *Making of a Filipino.* Manila: (privately published), 1985.

Corpuz, Onofre. *The Philippines.* Englewood Cliffs, N.J.: Prentice-Hall, 1974.

De Dios, Emmanuel, ed. *Analysis of the Philippine Economic Crisis.* Quezon City: University of the Philippines Press, 1984.

Denton, Frank H.. *Filipino Views of America*, Washington, D.C.: Asia Fellows Ltd., 1987.

Friend, Theodore. *Between Two Empires: The Ordeal of the Philippines, 1929-1946.* New Haven: Yale University Press, 1965.

George, T. J. S. *Revolt in Mindanao: The Rise of Islam in Philippine Politics.* New York: Oxford University Press, 1980.

Gowing, Peter Gordon. *Mandate in Moroland: The American Government of Muslim Filipinos, 1899-1920.* Quezon City: New Day Publishers, 1983.

_____. *Muslim Filipinos: Heritage and Horizon.* Quezon City: New Day Publishers, 1979.

Gowing, Peter Gordon, and Robert D. McAmis, eds. *Muslim Filipinos: Their History, Society, and Contemporary Problems.* Manila: Solidaridad Publishing House, 1974.

Grinter, Lawrence E. *Philippine Bases: Continuing Utility in a Changing Strategic Context.* Washington, D.C.: National Defense University, 1980.

Gross Holtz, Jean. *Politics in the Philippines*. Boston: Little, Brown, 1964.

International Studies Institute of the Philippines. *Muslim Filipino Struggle for Identity: Challenge and Response*. Selected documents for the Conference on the Tripoli Agreement, September 12–13, 1985. Quezon City: University of the Philippines Press, 1985.

Jenkins, Shirley. *American Economic Policy Toward the Philippines*. With an Introduction by Claude A. Buss. Stanford, Calif.: Stanford University Press, 1954.

Joaquin, Nick. *The Aquinos of Tarlac: An Essay on History as Three Generations*. Manila: Cacho Hermanos, 1983.

_____. *Doy Laurel in Profile: A Philippine Political Odyssey*. 2nd ed. Manila: Lahi, Inc., 1985.

Jurika, Stephen, Jr., and Edward A. Olsen. *Armed Forces in Contemporary Asian Societies*. Boulder, Colo.: Westview Press, 1986.

Kerkvliet, Benedict J. *Huk Rebellion: A Study of Peasant Revolt in the Philippines*. Berkeley: University of California Press, 1977.

Lachica, Eduardo. *Huk: Philippine Agrarian Society in Revolt*. Manila: Solidaridad Publishing House, 1971.

Lande, Carl. *Structure of Philippine Politics: Leaders, Factions, and Parties*. New Haven: Yale University Press, 1965.

Magno, A. R. *Nation in Crisis: A University Inquires into the Present*. Quezon City: University of the Philippines Press, 1984.

Majul, Cesar Adib. *Muslims in the Philippines*. 3rd ed. Manila: Saint Mary's Publishing, 1978.

Manchester, William. *American Caesar* (General MacArthur). Boston: Little, Brown, 1978.

Manglapus, Raul S. *The Philippines: The Silenced Democracy*. New York: Maryknoll, 1976.

Marcos, Ferdinand E. *Democratic Revolution in The Philippines*. Foreword by Carlos P. Romulo. 2nd ed. Englewood Cliffs, N.J.: Prentice-Hall International, 1979.

Martinez, Manuel F. *The Grand Collision: Aquino vs. Marcos*. Hong Kong: AP and G Resources, 1984.

Mijares, Primitivo. *Conjugal Dictatorship of Ferdinand and Imelda Marcos*. San Francisco: Union Square Publications, 1986.

Miller, Stuart Creighton. *Benevolent Assimilation: American Conquest of the Philippines:, 1899–1903*. New Haven: Yale University Press, 1982.

Paez, Patricia Ann. *The Bases Factor: Realpolitik of R.P.-U.S. Relations*. Manila: Center for Strategic and International Studies, 1985.

Pedrosa, Carmen Navarro. *Imelda Marcos*. New York: St. Martin's Press, 1987.

Phelan, John Leddy. *Hispanization of the Philippines: Spanish Aims and Filipino Responses, 1565–1700*. Madison: University of Wisconsin Press, 1959.

Poole, Fred, and Max Vanzi. *Revolution in the Philippines: The United States in a Hall of Cracked Mirrors*. New York: McGraw-Hill, 1984.

Quezon, Manuel Luis. *The Good Fight*. New York: D. Appleton-Century Co., 1946.

Quijano de Manila (Nick Joaquin). *The Quartet of the Tiger Moon: Scenes from the People-Power Apocalypse*. Manila: Book-Stop, Inc., 1986.

Quirino, Carlos. *Chick Parsons: America's Master Spy in the Philippines*. Quezon City: New Day Publishers, 1984.

_____. *Magsaysay of the Philippines*. Manila: Ramon Magsaysay Memorial Society, 1958.

Reyes, Narciso G., ed. *Foreign Relations Journal*. Vol. 1, no. 1. Manila: Philippine Council for Foreign Relations, 1985.

San Juan, Epifanio. *Crisis in the Philippines*. South Hadley, Mass.: Bergin and Garvey, 1986.

Scaff, Alvin H. *Philippine Answer to Communism*. Stanford, Calif.: Stanford University Press, 1955.

Schirmer, Daniel B., and Stephen Rosskaum Shalom. *The Philippines Reader*. Boston: South End Press, 1987.

Schurz, William Lytle. *Manila Galleon*. New York, E. P. Dutton, 1959.

Simbulan, Roland G. *Bases of Our Insecurity: A Study of the U.S. Military Bases in the Philippines*. 2nd ed. Manila: Balai Fellowship, Inc., 1985.

Stanley, Peter W. *A Nation in the Making: The Philippines and the United States, 1899–1921*. Cambridge: Harvard University Press, 1974.

Steinberg, David Joel. *The Philippines: A Singular and a Plural Place*. Boulder, Colo.: Westview Press, 1982.

_____. *Philippine Collaboration in World War II*. Ann Arbor: University of Michigan Press, 1967.

Taruc, Luis. *Born of the People* (Autobiography of the leader of the Huks). New York: International Publishers, 1953.

Wolf, Leon. *Little Brown Brother*. New York: Longman, Green, 1961.

Zaide, Gregoria F., and Sonia Z. Pritchard. *History of the Republic of the Philippines*. College ed. Manila: Manila National Bookstore, 1983.

ABOUT THE AUTHOR

Claude Buss's interest in the Philippines and his attachment to the Filipino people began in 1940 with his assignment as executive assistant to the U.S. High Commissioner there and has never abated. He has known most of the people mentioned in this book and has observed at firsthand both the campaign leading to Mrs. Aquino's election and the recent vote on the Constitution that reaffirmed her nation's confidence in her.

His career has combined teaching, writing, lecturing, and government service covering many years and many countries. After completing graduate work at the University of Pennsylvania and post-graduate work in Europe, he entered the United States foreign service and was posted to Peking and Nanking at the time that Chiang Kai-shek set up his national government and the Japanese began their invasion of the Asian mainland.

He returned to the United States to teach International Relations at the University of Southern California from 1935 to 1940, then began his tour of duty in Manila. When U.S. High Commissioner Frances B. Sayre was ordered to Corregidor along with General MacArthur, Claude Buss remained in Manila as the senior U.S. official left to face the Japanese. Interned in Manila and transferred to Tokyo by the Japanese, he was eventually returned to the United States, where he directed the San Francisco office of the U.S. Office of War Information.

In 1946, Professor Buss joined the faculty of the History Department at Stanford, where he taught classes on China, Japan, Southeast Asia, and U.S. Policy in Asia and the Pacific. While at Stanford he took a leave of absence to serve with General MacArthur during the occupation of Japan and also went on short-term missions to Korea, Taiwan, the Philippines, and other countries in Southeast Asia.

After retiring from Stanford in 1969, he taught at San Jose State University, and since 1976 has been Professor of Asian Area Studies in the National Security Department of the U.S. Naval Postgraduate School in Monterey as well as visiting scholar at the Hoover Institution. His most recent books are *National Security Interests in the Pacific Basin* and *The U.S. and the Republic of Korea: Background for Policy.*

Claude Buss has taught American history in the Philippines and Philippine history in the United States, twice as a Fulbright Exchange Professor; both governments have honored him for "service to the cause of Philippine-American friendship and understanding." A frequent traveler to the Philippines, he has made four trips in the year since Cory Aquino rose to power.

This volume is not just another tribute to President Aquino's accomplishments; it is an analysis by a longtime observer of the problems and possibilities facing the president, her administration, and the Filipino people.

CREDITS

Illustrations appearing on the following pages have been reproduced with the kind permission of the individuals and institutions listed.

Cover Page	AP/Wide World Photos.
8	Map drawn by Joan Melim.
14	AP/Wide World Photos.
38	Reuters/Bettmann Newsphotos.
94	AP/Wide World Photos.
100	From the library of the *Manila Chronicle,* courtesy the *Manila Chronicle.*
101	From the library of the *Manila Chronicle,* courtesy the *Manila Chronicle.*
106	Map drawn by Joan Melim.
112	From the library of the *Manila Chronicle,* courtesy the *Manila Chronicle.*
130	From the library of the *Manila Chronicle,* courtesy the *Manila Chronicle.*
133	From the library of the *Manila Chronicle,* courtesy the *Manila Chronicle.*
134	From the library of the *Manila Chronicle,* courtesy the *Manila Chronicle.*
150	From the library of the *Manila Chronicle,* courtesy the *Manila Chronicle.*
175	AP/Wide World Photos.
196	Photograph by Chuck Painter, Stanford News and Publications.

THE PORTABLE STANFORD

This is a volume in The Portable Stanford, a subscription book series published by the Stanford Alumni Association. Portable Stanford subscribers receive each new Portable Stanford volume on approval. Books may also be ordered from the following list.

Series Editor: Miriam Miller
Production Coordinator: Gayle Hemenway
Cover and Book Design: Mary Henry
Art Direction: Andrew Danish

To Order

e Copies

Yourself

a Friend,

Fill in

d Return

his Card.

☐ Please send me _____ copy(ies) of **Cory Aquino and the People of the Philippines** at $9.95 each (Calif. residents add .70 tax). Price includes shipping and handling.

NAME

ADDRESS

CITY, STATE, ZIP

☐ Please send _____ gift copy(ies) with gift card to:

NAME

ADDRESS

CITY, STATE, ZIP

☐ Payment enclosed.

Please allow 6–8 weeks for delivery.   BKIN

It's Easy

To Join

The

Portable

Stanford

st Fill in

d Return

his Card.

As a Portable Stanford subscriber you will receive a new PS title every three to four months. To keep the book, pay $9.95. If you don't wish to keep a book, simply place it back in its mailing carton and drop it in the mail (we pay return postage). Portable Stanford books are written by Stanford faculty on topics of interest to you, the curious, discerning reader with little spare time; each book is written and designed to be informative, entertaining, and highly readable. To join the PS family, just fill in the information below and send us this card.

☐ Please add my name to The Portable Stanford subscriber list. I understand that I will receive each new book in the series on approval.

NAME

ADDRESS

CITY, STATE, ZIP

☐ Please send me information on past Portable Stanford titles.   BKIN

BUSINESS REPLY MAIL
FIRST CLASS   PERMIT NO. 67   PALO ALTO, CA

POSTAGE WILL BE PAID BY ADDRESSEE

The Portable Stanford
Stanford Alumni Association
Bowman Alumni House
Stanford, CA 94305

BUSINESS REPLY MAIL
FIRST CLASS   PERMIT NO. 67   PALO ALTO, CA

POSTAGE WILL BE PAID BY ADDRESSEE

The Portable Stanford
Stanford Alumni Association
Bowman Alumni House
Stanford, CA 94305